The Time

of the

Bedouin

ALSO BY IAN DALLAS:

The Book of Strangers
The New Wagnerian
The Ten Symphonies of Gorka König
Collected Works (plays and prose)

Ian Dallas

The Time
of the
Bedouin

on the politics of power

BUDGATE PRESS

First edition: Budgate Press 2006
All rights reserved
www.budgatepress.com
info@budgatepress.com

Subject: Political Theory

ISBN: 0-620-37366-0

Printed by Formeset, Cape Town, South Africa

CONTENTS

to   Dugald Stewart Dallas

with   gratitude

for   "my heritage, Which my dead
father did bequeathe to me." (Shakespeare)

ὣς ὅ γε κοιρανέων δίεπε στρατόν· οἱ δ' ἀγορήνδε
αὖτις ἐπεσσεύοντο νεῶν ἄπο καὶ κλισιάων
ἠχῇ, ὡς ὅτε κῦμα πολυφλοίσβοιο θαλάσσης
αἰγιαλῷ μεγάλῳ βρέμεται, σμαραγεῖ δέ τε πόντος.

"And they streamed back again to the place
of assembly from their ships and their
huts, with a roar like that of the sounding
sea, when the breakers crash on a wide
open shore, and the deep sea thunders."

The Iliad, 2/207-210

(trans. Martin Hammond)

PART 1

I

A version of reality has been instituted which accords with the power élite's programmes of the expropriation of personal wealth, and its relocation in inter-connected corporate and statal structures. To further hide the venal truth of this oligarchy it has proved propitious to borrow the evaluations and vocabulary of the emergent scientific method of materialist evolutionism. As a result the world's ignorant masses have been presented with a model of reality that in itself is fictive and determinist at the same time. This binary model is crude but attractive to the uninformed, that is, the mass-educated workers, taking 'workers' to represent not the labouring class of Marx, but rather the all-inclusive definition of men as functioning under the constraints and enslaving force of technique – the delineation of Jünger in his key work, 'Der Arbeiter'.

The orthodoxy of the oligarchs divides history into two epochs and puts between them the force that split society into its two stages, and at the same time initiated the second historical phase.

The first stage of history (from this viewpoint) was the natural and 'primitive' society. From the moral point of view, everything about it was dreadful. It was presented as static. Its dominant condition was inescapable poverty for 'the people'. It was controlled and dictated to by hereditary rulers, kings and princes. They were by definition – that is, as princes and rulers – tyrants and oppressors. They taxed and made wars entirely for their dynastic benefit. Kings were despots, 'the people' were their helpless victims, poverty-stricken, famished and ground under by the pair of boots that trampled them – the Monarchy (the aristocratic élite) and the Clergy (also land-owners).

The second stage of history (from this

viewpoint) was the willed and legislated society. From the moral point of view it declared the emergence of the New Man, virtuous and imposing the good. It was presented as dynamic. Its dominant condition was the smashing of the enslaving monarchic and 'divinely ordained' system, and the creation of the new rule of man in a post-christian, that is, atheist condition. 'The people' ruled – power had passed to the formerly enslaved masses. The new leaders of society were liberators, dispensing justice and freedom. The first stage of history (the 'Ancien Régime') was ANCIENT. The second stage of history (la Révolution) was MODERN. From this point on we are in the modern world. 1789 is the new Dawn of Mankind. Indeed, within the unfolding of the Revolution there is the historical sense of a new beginning with the creation of a new calendar, a new Supreme Deity unifying all previous religions, and the inauguration of Year 1.

Elements of this modernism had already surfaced in England just over a hundred years before. It embodied the principle of abolishing monarchy and thus instituting regicide. It also offered the doctrine of the sovereignty of Parliament. The first element was softened by a Restoration which in turn was followed by a dynastic overthrow which installed a constitutional monarch. Thus the exile of James II marked the end of monarchic rule and saw the beginning of elected Assembly rule. It was never a people's parliament, however. The advent of King William meant the beginning of an aristocratic rule which was to survive until the end of the twentieth century. It was called and was claimed to be 'the Glorious Revolution', pretending by that to have been bloodless and popular. This was far from the truth. It entailed a bloodletting from Monmouth's Rebellion (while James II still ruled) to the ghastly slaughter by 'King Billy' in Ulster – itself a suffering that as of today still claims lives, but most tragically on to the continued struggle of the Jacobites to restore personal rule. This ended with the defeat of Bonnie Prince Charlie in 1745, which in turn led to the genocidal emptying of the Highlands by slaughter and slave-deportation to the colonies. The clans were driven out, bringing an ancient and noble culture to an end. This paved the way for 'Enlightenment' in Edinburgh and the Revolutionary theorists of the oligarchic usury élite.

This still could only be seen as a primary sketch of the new modernity – for it lacked the vital energising doctrine that was to see in the Modern

Age. The British 'Revolution' had been in the name of God. The French Revolution was in the name of Man.

Here was a Revolution without precursors. Even in the thinking of its exponents it was consciously viewed as a new beginning in the history of mankind. It ripped apart the fabric of time. It declared its repudiation of tradition and the past. It claimed that for the first time society was being created on rational principles. They were starting from zero. 1789 saw the emergence of a unified set of beliefs. The limitless power of the will. The efficacy of reason. The indefinite capacity to mould reality. It was not utopian. Political will could change reality and reconstruct society. This connection between willing and constructing constitutes the primal root of revolutionary terror. Therefore, the Terror does not date from 1793, nor even 1792 or 1791. It is consubstantial with the Revolution and emerges in 1789 as a pure adventure of the human will.

Terror is not a speciality of the French Revolution. It is a speciality of humanist and godless power. The importance of what happened from 1789–1794 is that it is a set of events which were to become the clear model of the new age's political system. The American Revolution has its own structural flaws and transformations, but although it prefigured the French adventure it could not escape a harmonic resonance with it. Their Government's first conflict was the Bankers' War which announced that the Revolution had unleashed its power. The genocide of the native American tribes or nations was the 'necessity' that the élite required to sustain their 'manifest destiny' – a political term used to define the American Republic and its global aspirations, yet clearly derived from French Revolutionary discourse.

The Revolution in 1789 had overthrown the sovereignty invested in an absolute monarchy, and then without changing its content set up that same absolutism in the hands of elected representation, but they did not merely remove the King of the 'Ancien Régime', with him went the ancient society of orders and bodies that had surrounded the King and were, in fact, the institutions which set limits and constraints on royal absolutism. The corporate structure of society, with its hierarchies and its privileges and its rights, imposed significant inhibitions on the King's power. All these obstacles to the royal will were swept aside on 4 August 1789. In their place the Revolution had set up a society of individuals, juridically equal but at the same time nakedly exposed to the direct action of the State.

Yet right at the beginning, as the Revolution's dynamic has been activated, it is also driven to manifest its inner counter-force, its necessary negative, without which it cannot realise its own nature and true face. It finds itself being interrogated from within itself. The question is that if the Revolution is the will of all the people, once achieved, what reason is there for it to continue? The inescapable answer within its own implacable logic is that if there are moves to dismantle it, to modify its claims, to abandon its projects, then this must be the 'evil' (for the people are intrinsically 'good') counter-revolution, that is the Revolution's mirror, its double, its other self. François Furet expressed it thus: "To the power of the People is posited a permanent anti-power, an omni-present matrix, like the nation, but hidden while it is public, specific while it is universal, evil while it is good. Its negative, its opposite, and its anti-principle."

Indeed, the Revolutionary is unthinkable independently of his enemy and secret necessity, the counter-revolutionary. They form an inseparable unity, for only the latter can provide the former with that licence he requires to take on the limitless extremities to which he will be driven. The 'enemy' which comes to dominate the Revolutionary discourse and then programme is 'the aristocrat'. Yet it is not even the aristocrat 'as such' – no, he is an icon, a target, an image – not one with a historical or even a financial silhouette. No, he is the embodiment of a social delineation that represents inequality. He is privileged. He is the zone of the socially unattainable to the masses. They cannot enter the Court. They cannot be high-ranking officers in the military. They are not taxed as others are taxed. The Revolution comes with equality – against it stands privilege. From this collision emerged the 'aristocratic plot', and fear of it produced yet another function of the Revolution. It became the index by which the nation itself was constituted and became aware of itself. In 1789 the almost spontaneous organisation across France of National Guards both gave body to the fear of the 'aristocratic plot' and at the same time gave character and personality to this new idea of the People as a community bonded together uniquely by possessing their newly won 'rights'. Patrice Gueniffey defined it as: "The re-invention of a community by the at least symbolic exclusion of a fraction of its members."

At the very point at which the activating force of a constant revolutionary process emerges – the necessary 'other' has to emerge as well. It must not be forgotten that this model of the modern world that is the French Revolution clearly manifests with the 'bourgeois' in Russia, the racial enemy in Germany, the 'enemies of the People' of Mao, and the phantom Jihadies of the US-Israeli axis today – so it is important that the true character of events today is understood in the light of the events leading up to France's cataclysm.

The great political theorist Montesquieu's argument had been that an independent hereditary aristocracy restrained the State in its unconditional will to power. At the beginning of the affair is the absolute monarch. From Louis XII to Louis XIV an emerging wealthy aristocracy began to flex its muscles. England had gone from a ruling monarch to a ruling aristocracy, hiding behind a pretended democratic frame, Parliament, in reality the new oligarchy's tool. France's similar bid to, not dethrone but limit the monarch, La Fronde, had been crushed. Had it succeeded, in all probability, France would have seen the same narrow, oligarchic spread of wealth that England had seen, even including their version of Henry VIII's dissolution of the monasteries into the coffers of the Dukes.

Absolute rule, as it is wrongly called, was set in a series of inhibiting and controlling institutions that did not really ever allow King in confrontation with either his subject or his State. Remember, it was under Louis XVI that torture was abolished. Not the case today, when it is the 'Revolutionary' democracies that have not only re-instated it, but made it more horrible: Britain in Ireland, Israel in Palestine, and the USA everywhere they have staked a claim.

The initial phase of the uprising, revolt that is, not yet a Revolution, came at the instigation and agitation of the bourgeois, thwarted by the 'ancien' rules from betterment, that is, those rules which barred them from Court and King. The lawyers, Danton and Robespierre, had changed their names to D'Anton and de Robespierre. They wanted to get on, and they wanted to get in. This frustration, when released, was to cause the deaths of hundreds of thousands. Brissot called himself Brissot de Warville. The layered society descended from King and Court (Versailles) to Aristocracy and Clergy, then peasants and city populace. Yet moving across these strata was a growing and greedy political force – the Bankers. Saint-Simon openly spoke up against Louis XIV's growing dependence on them, on seeing Louis escort

Samuel Bernard round the Château de Marly to talk him into a loan. The marriage in 1786 of the banker Necker to the Swedish diplomat De Staël was an event of State policy, and the contract was signed by the King and Queen and all the princes of the blood. In 1789 the great bankers who had always stood by the Monarchy, faced with the risk of a Government repudiation of the Debt, found themselves backing the Revolution if they, 'as the State', could guarantee payment. To this end they actively furthered the Revolution. Between 1750 and 1775 the value of industrial production doubled. Trade increased threefold. Colonial trade fivefold. Despite setbacks, in 1776-77 French trade and industry was in expansion.

The myth today taught in schools worldwide is that of a starving peasantry, unable to bear any more poverty and tyranny, finally turning on their tyrannical master and once and for all ending this old-fashioned, outdated system of monarchy, and declaring a new dawn of liberty, fraternity and equality. The French peasant never saw a degradation to equal that of the Brazilian peasants today, nor a Parisian bourgeois ever felt as stripped of wealth and possible growth equal to that of an Argentinean bourgeois today, and most definitely none of the French Aristocracy ever boasted an undeserved wealth to come anywhere near that of the nameless few hundred oligarchs of oil, media, weapons and finance who daily amass more billions from the world's poor.

Juarès, the early 20th century French socialist, wrote: "The Bourgeoisie is not merely a force of prudence and economy – it is a bold and conquering force that has already in part revolutionised the system of production and exchange, and is about to revolutionise the political system."

The Revolutionary statesmen, Barnave, openly admitted: "The whole of the French Revolution can be attributed to the progress of civilisation, enlightenment and industry, for it is this cause which, raising up the Third Estate and augmenting its wealth, education and self-respect, made a democratic revolution inevitable."

Therefore the Revolution did not come to relieve the oppressed masses – it was intended to bring 'democracy' to the affluent, not even to let an ambitious under-class grow more wealthy. In France, seigneurial privilege co-existed with a free peasantry, that peasantry owning between a third and a quarter of the land. The real enemy was the large landowner, sometimes noble but more often bourgeois or even yeoman farmer (laboureur), who threatened the peasant with expropriation. The Church, the First Estate, amounted to no more than 100,000, owned about one tenth of the land, and took further substantial income from tithes. It controlled its own finances and was exempt from taxation but made a significant quinquennial grant to the Crown which gave it financial pressure on the Government when it chose to withhold or reduce it. It controlled education and the pulpit was a national 'media' outlet. At the same time the new atheism had crept into catholic intellectuals' thinking. The Benedictine monastery of Saint Aubin at Angers sported busts of Voltaire and Rousseau, and several local clergy belonged to masonic lodges.

So it was that the France of the Ancien Régime was extremely complex. Since Louis XIV the monarchy had abdicated its role in many spheres to the aristocracy. The 'unfinished' Fronde was in motion again. With a newly ambitious aristocracy far from loyal to its royal source, and with the developing economic power of the middle class, alongside an insecure Church which in 1788 broke its traditional allegiance to the Crown to join in the aristocratic offensive against the Monarchy, the old structures, far from crumbling, were resistant to each other.

What proved the catalyst that fused the social tensions of the three blocks of French society into one all-engulfing explosion was the bankruptcy of the Monarchy. It must not be forgotten that the international banking community did constitute a fraternity, even a class, with a shared philosophy and practice. The great social theorist, Pierre-Joseph Proudhon, called them 'Le Secte'. This aspect of historical events has long gone un-noticed, and often has been deliberately obscured by the simple means of assuring that the academic paymasters of the historians commissioned them to preach the financial bank-based status quo. All English 'history' from Gibbon to Macaulay and Trevelyan has been 'Whig' history which, decoded, means pro-mercantile and 'free-trade' economy history. Far from being some kind of conspiracy of world banking, rather it indicates how central and unhidden their activities were, if, nevertheless, not at all understood. Yet right at the heart of the Revolutionary event it was ultimately understood in America, by the brilliant Benjamin Franklin, who had dandled his finger under the model guillotine on King Louis XVI's desk, ("Would a curved blade not be better, your Majesty?") before going on to discuss France's support for their Revolution. In due course the post-monarchic American State would face its first and unresolved political crisis, called 'the Bankers' War', which pitted the States against Federal Finance. It is not then an irony of history but a foundational fact of the crisis in France that its crisis came to a head under the burden of the so-called War of American Independence.

The Swiss banker, Necker, in control of France's economy from October 1776 to May 1781, was praised for raising loans successfully to defray war expenditure without increasing taxes to provide for their redemption and servicing. In 1781 he announced that there was a 'normal' annual surplus, exclusive of war expenditure, to the tune of 10 million livres. In fact, the American War left the Monarchy with a burden of debt in the region of 3,400 million livres plus an annual deficit of around 80 million. Louis, unprepared to repudiate the Debt, was forced to increase the taxation of the privileged orders. This allowed a perfect opportunity to win a final victory over the remains of royal absolutism by using the issue to force the King to accept an aristocratic constitution, in other words to evolve or devolve into an aristocratic oligarchy on the English model.

In 1783 Calonne was appointed Controller-General of Finance. By August 1786 he came up with a scheme which had to anticipate the large tranche of the American Debt due at the end of the year. It was a far-reaching scheme which included a re-evaluation of land. His proposed re-structuring of tax involved the abolition of the fiscal distinction between Terres Nobles and Terres Roturières, which would end seigneurial privileges of every kind, breaking the link of nobility to King. Land would be taxed as land only, not by type of ownership. Calonne was putting forward the basic financial view which by punishing the aristocracy opened the way to a bourgeois conception of society.

The forced dismissal of Calonne gave the aristocracy the very victory that in the end destroyed both them and their betrayed monarch. Archbishop Brienne became the new finance minister, backed by Clergy and aristocracy. Once it was clear that these two factions would not agree to rescue the Monarchy financially, even Brienne is said to have commented: "Since the nobility and the Clergy abandon their natural protector, the King, he will have to take refuge in the arms of the commoners." So it was that in the first months of 1789 open conflict had emerged between the nobility and the bourgeois Third Estate over the fragmenting power of monarchy. One such deputation of them turned up at Versailles trying to recruit more support from the Court. This forced the Government to lock them up in the Bastille, scarcely the residents that illustrious prison tells history it housed. They were, in fact, almost immediately released.

At the heart of the crisis, Brienne moved from failure to failure. By June 1788 he was forced to agree to the convocation of the Estates General by 1789. By August the royal government was on the verge of bankruptcy. Treasury payments were suspended for a month, and were to be made up partly in Caisse d'Escompte bank-notes, at the same time as the Caisse was relieved of its obligation to redeem its notes on demand. Disorder followed in Paris and Brienne was burned in effigy. In August the Archbishop gave his resignation to Louis. This left the King no choice but to recall Necker.

Necker, the banker, citizen of the Republic of Geneva, and a protestant – stood between the monarchy and the aristocracy. As Marie-Antoinette herself saw, well able to recognise the internal contradiction at the heart of the State: "The nobility will destroy us, but it seems to me that we cannot save ourselves without it."

There was turmoil among the aristocracy, between old families and new titles and the princes of the blood. At the same time the bourgeois Third Estate grew in confidence and in its emergent self-defining discourse. Madame de Chastinay found the Third Estate less disorderly and more attached to the person of the King than her own order. It was clear that the nobility's only concern was to preserve its own existence as a separate order in a hierarchical society. By May 1789 both Necker and the King still saw their threat as coming from them. The Séance Royale on 27 June was a charter for the aristocracy. The King was to be a constitutional monarch. He would be unable to raise taxes or loans without the Estates General. Ruling monarchy was to be abolished. The King had surrendered to them – but the dynamic did not lie with them alone.

In this atmosphere the new economic pulsation began to affect all of society. It was a capitalist phenomenon. The wealthy and privileged merchants called for the abolition of the Guilds. Now, the monarchically protected Guilds represented the historical bulwark against naked financial power and ownership. Their destruction was the true meaning of Charles I's beheading, never was it about theories of Divine Right. The same vital issue that now emerged was that in fact a new financial bourgeoisie required the transformation of free peasants and artisans into a wage-based working class.

On August 3, Malouet produced a Bill for the creation of a nation-wide system of employment and public assistance bureaux. Neither the Tiers-État of 1789 nor the Montagnards of 1793 intended to share political power with the artisan and the peasant. As Deputy Duquesnoy wrote of the People in June 1789: "Its happiness must be assured, but not by its own efforts."

Against the disastrous news of a failed harvest, all these conflicts spread and fragmented. Riots only could transform into Revolution when one group took control. When the bourgeoisie took it on themselves to restore order and did not turn to the King for protection, the fulcrum of State order was put out of action. The Marquis de Ferrières noted that the capitalists and Rentiers rallied to the support of the Assembly and employed in its defence all the powerful weapons of money, influence and connections.

When the crisis broke, the 407 Electors of the Paris deputation to the Estates General had their policies ready. They were wealthy and middle-class on the whole. At the 14 July meeting in the Hôtel de Ville, among the 379 Electors who turned up, 2 were members of the Academy, there were 5 deputies, 4 bankers, 26 merchants, 154 lawyers and 13 doctors. Down the social scale but still relatively prosperous were 43 retailers and 18 master-craftsmen. This was no oppressed mob of desperate peasants which set up a new National Guard to be the instrument of civic control. With relief, Deputy Duquesnoy noted that the new National Guard consisted of "a great number of really respectable people, some of the best citizens in town, Knights of St. Louis, Knights of Malta, very well-established bourgeois financiers and lawyers."

At the Assembly meeting on 4 August the revolutionary Breton Club invited liberal aristo-crats voluntarily to renounce some of their feudal privileges. The staged manoeuvre was highly successful and in a night of near-hysteria one after another from among the nobility surrendered benefit after benefit, feudal rights, hunting rights, seigneurial justice. Mirabeau commented on the session, "How like our Frenchmen. They spend a whole month quarrelling over syllables (defining the Declaration of the Rights of Man) and then in one night they overthrow the whole traditional order of the monarchy." Ferrières wrote later that the Assembly was like a band of drunkards, and at the height of the meeting's frenzy Lally-Tollendal sent a note to the floundering President, "They have lost all control of themselves. Suspend the Session!" Power had passed to the People, or rather, their 'representatives'.

On the 20th of December the Assembly voted to sell Crown lands and Church property to the value of 400 million livres, and it was against this security that the new State issued its own credit notes, the Assignats. The Revolution had its own currency. Gone was the golden Louis. This was the heart of the Revolution. The Terror was the price. The Church's property expropriated, it only needed the February 1790 abolition of the contemplative organisations to put an end to catholic France. The religion of the Revolution was atheism, but to sustain its atheism it needed in the end to invent a State theism. The Revolution, to exist, required a counter-revolutionary, so too the Revolution's atheism required a synthetic theism.

On the 19th of June, noble titles, armorial bearings and all the forms and trappings of nobility were abolished. During this time the zealous political Clubs began to dominate Assembly legislation. Danton's District of the Cordeliers, because of its growing power and its protection of Marat, found that the Districts had been dissolved. That was May 1790. The Cordeliers became a Club. Its emblem was the 'eye of vigilance', a symbol we were all to meet again on the US dollar.

Since the purpose of the Revolution was the total abolition of a political and social order it was not, could not be perceived as a political reality in opposition to another political reality. To all effects it was a war, unconditional, whose end could only be the total destruction of the Ancien Régime. The issue was so high, so elevated, liberty, equality, that it brooked of no compromise, no accommodation. It was non-negotiable and could only end with the utter destruction of 'the other'.

Edmond Burke realised at once that it was unlike any other revolution that had ever taken place in Europe. He noted: "It is a revolution of doctrine and theoretical dogma." He went on to observe that the last theoretical and doctrinal revolution had been the Reformation. One could usefully extend his analysis thus: the Catholic Church functioned under the élite of the clergy (the monasteries) who alone could administer the mystical sacrament. The Reformation abolished the élite priesthood by declaring the doctrine of the Priesthood of all Believers. The result of this was that the clerical élite gave way to the power of the University. This opened the way to so-called free-thinking. This in turn led to the Revolution which declared the Priesthood of all Unbelievers, the Citizens! It was the theology of humanism, and its Inquisition was to be Terror. There could be no opposition tolerated. Error was read as evil and evil was read as crime.

On 10 July 1791 Robespierre made a ferocious attack on those who opposed the dismissal of noble officers. "I must speak to you with a frankness that seems rude, but the circumstances demand it. Whoever does not see the necessity of their dismissal is a fool. Whoever does see it and does not want it and does not propose it – is a traitor!"

Patrice Gueniffey argues that this absolutism of political conflict is what was to open the door to all the excesses and all that resulted, and so was co-extensive with the Revolution. "With the revolutionary 'constructivism', with the unitary conception of sovereignty and the quest for transparent power, with the obsession of the plot and the egalitarian passion," he observes, "it follows that what the Revolution concealed from its very beginning was violence and potential terror." Alessandro Manzoni wrote in 'The French Revolution of 1789 and the Italian Revolution of 1859': "From 1789 the Terror was in the French Revolution like a black spot on the skin of the fruit which announces the worm which gnaws at its interior."

Gueniffey announces Marat's emergence with his newspaper 'The Friend of the People' as the arrival of the herald of the Terror. It was 12 September 1789. The ferocity, the laying-down of the terms on which battle will be waged, here all at once was the annunciation of the Terror as surely as the opening chords of a Beethoven symphony presage all that is to come. The Deputies are cowards. The Monarch ambitious. The public enemy is enraged. There is 'a powerful faction hidden at the very heart of the Estates General'. The plot is everywhere, in the Court, in the Army, in the Paris Commune, even the Assembly itself. Marat announced the fateful solution. It was to purge ruthlessly, to eradicate, and to slash at those toxic weeds that persisted in growing back again. "The air," he declared, "is only cleared by storms."

What was once fought and won by lance, sword and cannon, in the Revolution was won by the media. It was by pamphlets and the press that victory was assured. Marat's paper was not alone. There were 'The Watchers', 'The Denouncers', and the sinister 'The Blind Clairvoyants'. To Marat the guillotine was not enough. He called on his readers to put the enemies of the Nation to the sword. Stone them. Stab them. Shoot them. Hang them. Burn them. Impale them. Quarter them. To the pardoned, he recommended that their ears be cut off and their thumbs sliced off for easy future recognition.

When he called for "Some heads to roll" with the spread by the media of the message, in reality it meant several thousand. In July 1790 he was complaining that five hundred guilty had not yet been executed to assure the Nation's happiness. A month later the number had risen to six hundred, this was to leap to twenty thousand and with the fall of the Monarchy the number to be eliminated had leaped to two hundred and seventy thousand traitors. Marat insisted that this was a humanitarian duty when one considered that the Counter-Revolution had already executed twenty thousand patriots, and was sworn to wipe out another five hundred thousand more. The media, that is the

Revolutionary press, newspapers and pamphlets, did not just denounce enemies of the People, it sowed suspicion and unease, its power was innuendo, distrust and denunciation by linkage of the innocent to the guilty.

It is not possible to fail to grasp that what happened then is happening now. The Bankers' Revolution, the doctrinally pure inheritor of its 1789 patriarch, today has been using the same media tactics. Destruction of a person's life or an innocent organisation's existence only require the published linkage of their name to the 'terrorists' of their new dialectic which has so cleverly transferred their practice of terror to the theoretical name for Islam, recycled in the press as the vehicle of terror itself.

The end result, then as now, was to reduce politics to the permanent exercise of suspicion. Patrice Rolland wrote in 1789: "It is remarkable to note to what point the citizen is absorbed into being controlled. There is such a truly political passivity that it reveals to what a degree power remains totally exterior and foreign to the citizen. [...] There is no place with Marat for a culture of participation and consultation."

The discourse of Marat indicated that the terror must end up with the dictatorship of the most virtuous and at the same time that it is condemned to be perpetual. This was to emerge again in the 20th century when Mao announced the Doctrine of Perpetual Revolution. This reveals in turn that the very Rousseau-esque doctrine of the recovery of the good men is rejected. The guarantee of the Terror's continuity becomes the guarantee of liberty.

In July 1789 Brissot is already justifying the need to have a category of the enemy which cannot be defined within the frame of 'citizenship'. He insisted that these evil enemies of the Revolution had to be dealt with as special cases, for the sake of 'public safety'. "The police, the committee of safety and its investigations were precisely created to meet these special cases. They have been armed with exceptional powers in order to prevent the flight of the conspirators."

Thus the function of Revolutionary government became to legislate means of exception, so that the legal definition of the enemy person as being rendered unfit for the process of law, guaranteed to the 'People' – that they had rendered the police procedure, the judgment and the execution carried out on these non-persons free of the scrutiny of the law and indeed the People – a juridic legitimacy. Once the person was defined as an outlaw, literally outside the reach of the law, then to eradicate them the State itself had to outlaw itself so as to remain unaccountable. Yet at that moment the pretence of high philosophy, of the rational, of universal justice and freedom, collapsed – cynical and brutal pragmatism took its place. Brissot frankly invoked Machiavelli: "Remember," he challenged Clermont-Tonnerre, "the trivial but true axiom: who wishes the end, wishes the means."

And so across Europe and the United States the way was paved by legislation to exempt from legislation – and here our current Revolution goes to the Marat limit of the irrational – not only those categorised as 'terrorists' but those who might be deemed probable in the future to commit 'terrorist acts'. And just as from 1789 laws that were initially aimed at the aristocratic conspirators within the year were to include commoners and even Deputies, so today the laws that were aimed at 'terrorists' soon swept up in their savagery innocent youths on the other side of the world from the new conspiracy, as well as other innocents with only a racial or religious connection. No-one in France was safe in 1789. Not one

Muslim out of two billion was safe in the global reach of the 2002 Revolution. Terror reached out to the American citizens with the Patriot Act and by military and intelligence operations, into the mountains of Afghanistan, East Turkestan, and the streets of Jakarta and Sydney.

Roberto Martucci recognised that the monarchic social order protected itself with a little-used and ill-defined legal term, Lèse majesté, from a criminal ordinance of 1670. He identified clearly the logical trap into which the Revolution had fallen. François de Pange admitted that national sovereignty had to be recognised in the same manner as royal sovereignty. The Nation could not be sovereign until it had taken to itself this 'privileged instrument of oppression'. In 1788 Augeard accused the Garde des Sceaux Lamoignon of the crime of Lèse-Nation. Elsewhere they called it Lèse-État.

The cutting-free of the legal framework and any kind of juridical philosophy took (and takes) place in a plethora of politically dictated special measures, and this in parallel with the high rhetoric of the Rights of Man which is upheld as being 'that which must be preserved' by the setting-apart from mankind of the 'evil enemy'.

41

The absolutist nature of law based on a Constitution, far from guaranteeing a form of justice, enhances the punitive power of the State. An accusation brought to court by a Constitutional charge constitutes in itself an inescapable pre-judgment. The fulfilling of the Constitutional strictures implies the guilt of those who stand accused. Solzhenitsyn in his classical de-construction of the modern state, 'The Gulag Archipelago', lays bare the chilling reality of how the Constitution itself is the genocidal instrument. He explains how the Constitution granted to each census district of a city the right to apprehend, under legally granted special powers, a certain number of suspects, for interrogation and sentencing, that number representing in every case the same percentage of that district's population. Thus, in one district they were allowed to arrest 200 suspects of crime against the State. When the local police chief found that only 10 had been brought in, he felt he had not 'fulfilled his Constitutional quota', and so sent out his forces to arrest another 190 people.

As in Revolutionary Paris, so in Stalin's Moscow, but so also in Parliamentary Britain. Britain, whose Medieval Kings upheld their proudest legal achievement, the Habeus Corpus law, under parliamentary rule has legislated a

'Terrorism Act' which permits the arrest even of those deemed liable to commit such a crime in the future. In democratic Britain from 1 September 2001 up to 31 March 2006 there were –

out of 997 arrested:
154 charged under Terrorism Act
175 charged under different Acts
25 convicted under Terrorism Act

In the USA in 2005, 6,000 were arrested and detained and held inaccessible to lawyers. Today the totalitarian system, called democracy, surpasses its historical predecessors. The lesson for the State today is that these Constitutionally legal emergency-power sweeps, rapidly fill up the prisons. The emergency solution then logically demands a rapid clearing of prison populations, by massacre, to make way for more. In our time this has been common practice in Pinochet's Chile, Reagan's San Salvador and Bush-Blair's Iraq and Afghanistan. It is only a political step away in England, France and Germany – again. Prison-emptyings by massacre and deportations are recorded democratic practices, as in the lethal genocidal 'Highland Clearances' and the mass killings of the French Republic again in 1848. In the February of that year, Louis-Phillipe, after having tried every means to find a political solution to the crisis, called in Marshal Bugeaud. The Marshal, fresh from his experience of 'pacification' in Algeria, insisted that to restore order in Paris and thus save the Crown, it would need the massacre of at least twenty thousand people. Louis-Phillipe refused, and lost the Crown. When he later heard the news of the bloody repression let loose by the Second Republic, he bitterly noted: "A Republic is lucky. It is able to fire on its own people!" So, too, the Paris Commune of 1871 was to be crushed with a bloody savagery never practised on the people by its Kings.

The summer of 1791 marks the turning point of events in the Revolution. The 16th of May saw a decree forbidding the re-election of constituents, assuring in one move a new ruling élite and at the same time the political liquidation of the aristocracy. On June 21 the royal family were arrested at Varennes, marking the official end to the King's executive power and at the same time the Assembly's assumption of Constitutional power. On July 9 a law was issued ordering all emigrants to return within a month on pain of being declared traitors in the event of an invasion. The door had swung quietly open onto the full storm of the Terror.

II

No historical subject has been submitted to more intense critical scrutiny in search of an explanation, indeed of an excuse, than the emergence in its fullness of that Terror which imposed itself in all its bloody ferocity from 1791. The necessity, for those who embrace the myth of modernity, that is the democratic principle which both governs the masses absolutely and at the same time places the wealth system out of access to government, is to explain the Terror, not to exonerate it, nor even to regret it.

The defendants of this indefensible political system, political democracy, are in an impossible situation. The excuse of one party is to insist that given the forces opposing the transformation of society by the Revolution, there was no alternative if the social project was to be saved. Yet that transforms the self-styled active force of the Revolution into the passive reaction to necessity.

In the politically endorsed summary study of the Bi-Centenary, 'L'État de la France pendant la Revolution', the hedging about of any possible 'explanation' for the Terror, coupled with the uneasy inability to commit to the statistics and details and extent of the genocide, makes for disturbing reading. In the end it simply is projected as the 'price' for 'our freedom'. Mona Ozouf noted in her re-assessment of events, one of those historians now finally asking and answering the difficult questions, that there were two polar opposite responses: resignation to necessity on the one hand, and wilful triumphalism on the other. In the one case, the Terror was a violent remedy imposed by an extreme peril but fundamentally alien to the Spirit of the Revolution which brought emancipation with the Rights of Man and universal suffrage. In the second case, without denying the reactive nature of the Terror, the Revolution found in it the means to rise beyond itself and achieve a new grandeur. To the first group the link between Revolution and Terror is accidental, and to the second it is almost necessary.

The issue reveals itself as being, not the presentation of the evidence of justification, but rather the viewing of the Revolution as one permitting it in the end to take its place as the acceptable foundational event of 'modernity'. Edgar Quinet has demonstrated that chronology does not admit a cause and effect view of the Terror as a reaction to menacing events. In Lyons the Terror was unleashed by Fouché and Collot d'Herbois well after the rebels had surrendered. Nantes was recovered by General Canclaux in June 1793 but Carrier and his executioners did not institute the mass drownings until December 1793. The army of the Vendée was cut in pieces at Mans in December 1793 but it was not until early 1794 that the horrific extermination of the populace was undertaken. As Quinet observed: "The Terror appeared almost everywhere after the victories. Are we saying that in our system the effect precedes the cause? We must if we intend to maintain that the Terror was necessary to produce the Republican victories which had preceded the Terror!" Both the massacres at Lyons and the genocide in La Vendée are the direct result of the initiatives of legally appointed representatives, whose decisions entail matters of power struggle, ambition and personal interest, all of which are the very lifeblood of the system of representative assembly government.

The procedures which gave legality and indeed were the legality on which Terror was founded have not in any way been surpassed in more recent democratic political procedure and practices. A constitutional instrument of power is itself a dynamic which can move into special modes, crisis policies, emergency powers, rules of exception. Such powers, far from being rare, are constants of 'democratic' governance, which allows us to say, however illogical it demonstrably is, that totalitarian edict and Terror are both built into and necessary for the continuance and survival of the same democratic system.

The whole web of 'discriminatory' edicts of the Third Reich were imposed with the total acquiescence of the citizenry to whom they did not apply. The Stalin 'Show Trials' were played out to the people in filmed sessions that were passively accepted. Roosevelt's special powers in the '30s Depression and later in World War II (when tens of thousands of innocent Japanese-born citizens were flung into prison camps) were inside the frame of a Constitution which but for special political legislation would have barred these policies. The very 'legality' of military conscription initiated in World War I, when the democracies were running out of men to kill, itself an outrage against individual liberty, once ensconced in legal protocol was never removed after the War and was all bright and ready to abscond with a new, unprotesting generation in 1939.

Look at Danton's famous discourse in the midst of the Terror. On March 9, 1793 he declared: "It is important to take judiciary measures to punish counter-revolutionaries, as it is for them that this Tribunal is necessary. It is for them that this Tribunal must yield to the supreme tribunal of the People's vengeance. ... Let us do what the legislative assembly did not do – let us be terrifying to save the People from having to be." These words have been most precisely echoed by an American President and a British Prime Minister prior to legislating away the exalted values of their respective States, while remaining firmly stationed inside the democratic discourse – since it does date from Danton himself.

The doctrine of the Terror as necessary product of circumstance is actually a post-Thermidorian creation erected by the surviving members of the Committee of Public Safety to distance themselves from Robespierre as they in turn began to be denounced as accomplices of 'the Tyrant'. From 26 to 29 August 1794, exactly one month after Robespierre's execution, Fréron, Tallien and Lecointre launched their attack on the Committee of Public Safety, themselves forced to turn their judicial challenge to Terror into a new Terror required to end that of Robespierre.

The war launched by the Revolution in 1792 began with trivial causes. Gueniffey notes that most historians now agree with Juarès that the war, far from being provoked by foreigners, was initiated by the Revolution, and that, for personal motives of survival and not for Revolutionary messianic motives.

Albert Sorel observed that the Revolution which removed the Bourbons in attacking the Hapsburg monarchy while doctrinally logical nevertheless reopened the old monarchic struggle to establish sound geographical frontiers (the Rhine, the Alps), and so the 'new' Revolution transformed into the 'old' struggle. However, the menace of Revolutionary force lay not with its then feeble army but with its universalist pretensions.

Alexis de Tocqueville saw it clearly.

"Every civic and political revolution has been enclosed in a country. The French Revolution had no territory as such. More than that, its effect was to wipe out all the old frontiers on the map. It was seen to unite or divide men despite their lands, their traditions, character or language. It opened up, above nationality, an intellectual country common to the men of all nations who could be its citizens. Search through the annals of history and you will not find a single political revolution which had the same character: you will only find it in certain religious revolutions.

"The French Revolution is thus a political revolution which operated, as it were, and took on the aspect of, a religious revolution."

Let us return to the eruption of the Terror in its full fury from inside the body of the Parliament. The Laws of Exception designed to prevent the departure of the Royals and High Aristocracy represented, according to Gueniffey, the opening of Pandora's Box and the unleashing of the Terror.

The Terror was not let loose by a mob in the streets howling for blood, although that became one of its by-products. It was generated by a series of laws, constitutional amendments and majority committee decisions, they themselves soon to become unanimous, such was the fear that dissension spelled treason and execution.

The enclosing, inhibiting and finally punitive legislation was all couched in the language of Rights, Freedoms and Tolérance. It was in the name of liberty, of conscience, that the Revolution guaranteed the liberty of religion. Once the atheist (secular) state was given oath of allegiance, a 'new' and 'protected in rights' Catholic clergy would be permitted. A permitted clergy, paid by the State and under oath of obedience to it, could 'freely practise' its holy rites. This in effect legislated the abolition of the Roman Catholic faith. The submission of religion to a ruling atheist (secular) state was the prior necessity to the introduction of a state religion (the Supreme Being) which transformed the political rulers into mystically sanctioned masters of men, as coronation once sanctified Kings.

It is precisely this process that is being re-enacted by the French capitalist State today. No need to smash Catholic wealth and power today – that had been done, that was effected by the Revolution's 'Édit de Tolérance' in 1789. Today the same process is being applied to the Muslims. Already a national grid of Imams is being set up. The training of Imams also implies not only State allegiance but a 'reformed' doctrine of Islam, with its necessary condition of abolishing Tawhid, since power has passed from Allah, say they, to the People. It is in this light that one may begin to understand the present world system's categoric rejection of allowing history studies into the educational frame. The cynicism of the political class could not be more clearly demonstrated than in the current anti-Muslim legislation – the French politicians know that this is a re-enactment of the Revolutionary process, yet it is nowhere admitted.

The law of separation of Church from State, that is of subjugation of Church to State, was vetoed by Louis XVI when the Legislative proposed it on 19 December 1791. On 27 May 1792 the Assembly submitted the law and again Louis XVI rejected it, but the fall of the Throne meant that by 26 August 1792 the laws could be enacted. Priests who did not submit a primal oath to the State were ordered to leave the national territory within two weeks, failure to comply entailed deportation to Guyana, the over-sixties and the sick to be imprisoned. 2004 saw the first expulsion of a Muslim Imam, citizen, for refusing to deny known Islamic injunctions. His expulsion took place in a barrage of media attacks very similar to the emotional slanders against the christian Church by the French Pamphlets of the Revolution.

There was no conspiracy by Clergy and Aristocracy to overthrow the Revolution despite their resistance to it. It was the repression of the State against them that transformed their various activities into a single conspiracy. By 1794 the victims of the Revolutionary Tribunal were not guillotined because they were guilty, but rather they were guilty because they had been guillotined. In 1791 the repression did not respond to a threat but rather by putting together presumptions of guilt, isolated acts and in themselves powerless oppositions, managed to construct a fantastic narration of enmity and danger which called for dreadful and punitive measures. In the words of the Revolution's Pamphlet, Moniteur, "Their inaction perhaps actually hides a profound deception."

Brissot openly promoted this political approach when on 30 December 1791 he declared to the

Jacobins: "Gentlemen, I must admit that I have only one fear, that is that we will NOT be betrayed. We have need of great betrayals, thus we can finish with the strong doses of poison that menace France." War against the German princes was for the Revolution 'some kind of solution'. War allows the hatred of an enemy to be the prior necessity to brutalise the one suspected of treason. Democratic France's systematic slaughter and torture was authorised in first Morocco then Algeria, then in Indo-China. Democratic Argentina was able to participate in creating a generation of Desparacidos. Viet Nam and Cambodia were to see the still undocumented horrors of Agent Orange and its genetic havoc, torture, the napalm bombing of villages, and the hundreds of soldiers summarily shot, dropped from helicopters, mutilated and buried alive – all this from the world guardian of the Revolution's doctrines of Democracy, Human Rights and Universal Suffrage, the United States of America. It was a policy that was to be applied in the next century from El Salvador and Iraq to Somalia and Afghanistan.

The fury of democratic war has to turn inward also, and punish the traitors who oppose war and its policies. Thus Isnard, 31 October 1791: "The application of this rigour is a terrible price when used by a tyrant to perpetuate tyranny, but when these means are employed by the entire body of the nation, they are not guilty. It becomes a great act of justice, and the Legislators who do not adopt these means become themselves guilty. For by political liberty to pardon the crime is to share in it. This rigour will cause blood to flow, I know it. But, if you do not shed it, will not even more blood flow? One must sever the gangrened limb to save the rest of the body."

In the devastating assessment of Gueniffey, "The Terror led to the war, and the war to the Terror." His conclusion marks the end of the collusion by French historians with the myth of the Revolution as a political liberator. The conclusion could not be more damning. He summed up: "The repressive laws of 1791 and 1792 by which the Terror wrote itself for the first time into the legislative arsenal, found in effect their justification in the contractual representation of the social order: they constitute by this fact a sort of counterpoint to the Declaration of the Rights of Man, of which they are an evidentiary negation, but with which they share a common origin."

On July 9, 1791, Barbère outlined very vividly the manner in which the social contract as guarantee of individual liberty became in special circumstances the suspension of liberty. "Once a 'free country' finds its existence threatened, the safety of the people becomes the supreme law. Before the necessities of public safety the Rights of Man must bow low respectfully."

Thus it is clear that the path to the Terror was not an anarchic road of increasing panic, disorder and fury but rather a carefully planned and legislated path, which once the political paradox had been accepted as reasonable, took the populace and the government into the zone of Terror as practice. That Terror as practice had not then emerged from a commitment to Terror as theory, rather it was the bloody offspring of anti-terrorist legislation. This in itself goes some way to explaining the numbing passivity with which the 'People', that great entity which nevertheless is void of existential reality, consented to the wholesale slaughter and savagery of the Terror. It is this role of the Revolutionary masses which destroys Michelet's thesis irrecoverably. Soviet man accepted the Gulag, Hitler's superior race turned away from the concentration camp network. Although dis-similar as States, each had in place a complex body of legislation which if applied opened up a category of non-person which in turn removed the sting from such a person's liquidation. These three historically distinct States nevertheless emerged as post-theistic entities, thus coming under the Dostoevskian realisation that if God did not exist, everything was permitted. Humanism, that is atheism, only requires a constitutional justification to give that permission. This situation is now the norm in both Europe and the USA. The 'laicité', the secularisation of the State abolishes religion, since religion can only exist as a social entity under Divine orders. 'Religio' means to-bind-together. Once religion is redefined as a personal belief system it has actually been reduced to a mere psychological condition. The French State became a worship-less Catholicism, and with its moral law abolished. The same definition applies to Hitler's post-Lutheran State, and Lenin's post-Orthodox State.

The re-structuration of the supra-national or indeed post-national State leads us to the recognition that what is at present taking place is the classical modus operandi of Revolution itself. The passivity, even indifference of the mass before the legislation that removes independence to replace it with social safety, the configuration of an exterior enemy, itself wittily named Terrorism, the appearance of a leadership that 'takes over' the machinery of State even with the appearance of being the elected government – all these elements emerging in unison must be inescapably the event called Revolution.

Today it is the liberal society of the 20th century that has finally been overthrown in the convulsions of two World Wars – Nolte saw them as one European Civil War which ended (twice) with an invasion by the military might of the USA. The monarchs are abolished, or tolerated on bicycles, or as celebrities, voided of political influence let alone action. With them have gone the remnants of a christian-based morality. Marriage has been replaced with 'the relationship', leaving legitimacy as an irrelevance. It is this last which lifts the veil on what we must call the current Revolution. Its transformation is to take to itself all private wealth and that means also property.

When banking was introduced into post-Osmanli Greece they found that, in a language that claims a word for everything, there was no word for 'bank'. The Orthodox Papas asked for a definition of its function. They were told that when the husband returned home he placed all his money on the table. The wife then divided and distributed the money. Some for food. Some for clothing. Some to pay a debt. Some for the children and some for entertainment. That, explained the new élite, is our affair. The Papas announced the Greek work for bank – it was 'a table'. Trapeza tys Hellados – the Bank of Greece – is in fact the Table of Greece.

More sinister was the decision that, by this definition, followed. The family table had to be abolished – for it was a private bank. Once the bank had the family money, then it followed that they would become debtors. In place of marriage, a remnant of Divine worship practice, came 'the relationship', itself a commercial term.

Alongside this revolutionary event was another, the expropriation of all significant land and properties. To this end death-duties were dutifully legislated after 1945 to guarantee the de-construc-tion of the old land-based aristocracy that had ruled over all Europe up until that time. Bank loans soon closed down the family chateau. Openly named 'Land Bank', the Sect quickly endebted the farming class. Quixotic farm-subsidies only delayed the inevitable, for as the bankers grew more powerful they soon re-designed state structures to be unified entities, so that what neither France nor England would do, Europe must.

The genetic modification of plants as an issue has proved one of the cleverest instruments of transformation by the banking élite. What it veils from the masses is that land is passing from private (farmers') hands to that of Corporations operating on the other side of the world. The G.M. issue has to resolve itself under the absolutism of the modern, yet the antique selfishness of the land grab will have been brilliantly hidden.

It is nearly impossible to de-construct the present situation without a historical recognition, an identification of Ur-forms which were not just set up in the French Revolution but have repeated themselves with such clarity in later Revolutions. Gueniffey has proposed the definition for our time: "...to define the Terror as the necessary product of the Revolution considered in itself, that is to say as a particular form of historical change, independent of its principles and even the place and the moment it breaks out. In other words, if the ideology becomes identified with the victims of the violence, it is still independently of their principles or of their objectives that revolutions produce, and necessarily produce, their victims."

Augustin Cochin, now that almost a century's events have given evidence as to the exactness of his analysis, has taken a central place in the current discourse. He recognised two ways of writing the history of a democratic régime. The first leans on the legal State, on declared principles, public programmes – a history easy to construct because one finds it 'on stage', its model well presented, well lit, stylish. The second consists of not looking at what is 'on stage', but rather looking 'in the wings', that is to say not the facade of official history but the practice and the real history of democracy.

Gueniffey sums up Cochin's position as being that democracy is a swindle, and that its advent announces an age of voluntary slavery, and confirms that "democratic participation rests on a presumption of universal competence, which, linked to the postulate of the spontaneous production of a collective will, represents a double fiction of which the effect is a transfer of power, theoretically possessed by the individuals, to an oligarchy composed of political professionals."

Joan Didion's critique of modern American democracy confirms the bleakest views of Cochin. She describes people inside the political and media process as "constituting a self-created and self-referring class, a new kind of managerial elite."

"When we talk about the process, we are talking, increasingly, not about 'the democratic process,' or the general mechanism affording the citizens of a state a voice it its affairs, but the reverse: a mechanism so specialised that access to it is correctly limited to its own professionals ... to that handful of insiders who invent, year in and year out, the narrative of public life."

"Who cares what every adult thinks," she quotes a Republican strategist telling the Washington Post in September 1998. "It's totally not germane to this election."

The view that at the heart of Revolution is a Jacobin entity implies a powerful rejection of all political theories that try to construct an improvisational model of an uncontrollable flux, a spontaneous uprising, even a natural evolution. It means that there is at the heart of Revolution a willed force, and therefore a nucleus of men prepared to impose their will. Ironically it is the Carlylian view of an uncontrollable flux hurtling to its end which is the determinist view, and the view of a party or a group who actively catapult that apparently anarchic flux which indicates an open vision of societal events.

Michelet in his 'Histoire de la Révolution Française' first used the term 'a political machine'. He defines it thus: "In the absence of a voluntary association which would give a living unity to the Revolution, an artificial organisation was needed, a league, a conspiracy, which would at least give a kind of mechanical unity. A political machine was necessary."

This is the same political apologist for the Revolution who with equal candour declared:

"Every history of the Revolution up to now was essentially monarchic. This is the first one that is Republican, which has smashed the idols and the gods. From the first page to the last it has had only one hero: the People."

This is the deception, the fundamental lie at the heart of all revolutionary, therefore democratic theory and thus practice. Again Gueniffey: "Democracy proposes the great number, while government requires the little number."

It is as if politicians have tried to make complex, veiled, and beyond us, what is inescapably simple and against us. He goes on: "The more the citizens are invested with an important, theoretical power, the less they exercise real influence."

It follows from this that the more elitism is denounced as being undemocratic, the more it can be recognised that a new élite is being set up under the smokescreen of an attack on an already defunct prior élite.

For example, since 1950 in Britain a systematic dissolution of the landed gentry was set in motion. Death duties wrenched from their hands the aristocratic 'Place', the country houses from which Britain had been ruled since 1688 and brought about the abolition of active monarchy. A 'National Trust' was set up with the intention of 'making accessible to the people' the great houses which it absorbed, one after the other, as, bankrupted, the historical owners yielded up their role of gentry. From being the social network of the oligarchy that controlled Britain, these houses passed into a subsidised limbo which reduced them to play parks with boat-rides and vintage motor shows. Cliveden, Blenheim, Kedleston, Woburn, Longleat. There, where once statesmen lorded it over the bankers, now the financial system of these once banker guests saw to it that centres of political power were forced out of action. In Punch on 22 January 1947 the cartoon showed a vast pillared drawing room in which the Lord of the Manor warned his son, "This is my last warning, Charles. If you do not mend your ways I shall leave the estate to you instead of the National Trust."

D.H. Lawrence in 'Lady Chatterley's Lover' wrote (1930):

"…and one by one, the stately homes, they were abandoned. Now they are being pulled down. … This is history. One England blots out another."

Having identified the Jacobin entity, Gueniffey goes on to isolate the nature of the Jacobin discourse. Our intention is to read his historical analysis as applicable to our present concerns, and in doing so, we are drawing the conclusions he not only inferred but had been indicating all along. He states:

"The Jacobin Discourse on sovereignty and the individual is a discourse on revolution, and more precisely on revolution as total war, with no other outcome than 'victory or death'. In reality this discourse is on *democracy at war*, a discourse which takes the principles of democracy – the individual, liberty, the government of law, the distinction between public and private – to a point of intensity at which it ends by inverting all these into their opposites."

Tocqueville observed that war killed democracy. Not only because it increased the powers of civil government, but also because in accustoming the people to violence and constraints, it leads 'gently' to despotism. War signifies regimentation, the abdication of every autonomy and all individual reason: it creates 'a social order in which the individual no longer exists,' but in which the individuals, in renouncing themselves, in abdicating all that separates and distinguishes them from each other in normal times, stripped of every particularity, achieve an absolute equality. The 'Jacobin Discourse' is a theory of the democratic individual plunged into war, that total war without any possible negotiated exit which is the Revolution itself. In the final viewpoint, Tocqueville, Furet, Gueniffey and Champion concur: "The Terror is a fate, not of the French Revolution but of every revolution considered as a modality of change. While revolutions are for the most part ideologically incomparable, they are however politically comparable."

It follows from this that what has been named the

Jacobin Discourse is itself the motor energy of the Revolution which drives it through its own radicalisation towards, inevitably, a violence which by its increase makes that radicalism of the day the moderation of the next day. The Revolution in France defined the idea of modern revolution as permanent, independent of ends, and investing legitimacy in the most radical of its actions. Thus the dynamic of revolution is analogous to the pure logic of war as defined by Clausewitz: "...War is an act of force, and there is no logical limit to the application of that force. ... Lastly, even the outcome of a war is not always to be regarded as final."

The French Revolution in its Terror moved from the mutual slaughter in Paris of political individuals to the genocide of a people, but the philosophy of slaughter remained constant: first define the enemy as a non-person, then eliminate. In the first phase a person was the victim, in the second, a whole people. June 2, 1793, Legandre called out: "Come down, or I will slaughter you!" to Lanjuinais who refused to leave the Tribune, and who hurled back the retort: "Decree that I am a bull, then you can slaughter me." The rhetoric of murder soon swept into the extremity of genocide: once defined as non-human or animal they could be removed. The people of La Vendée were declared a herd of pigs, a banished race. Barère referred to 'the inexplicable Vendée'.

The ghastly extermination of the Vendée, its men, women and children, remains a crime that Republicans prefer that we ignore or forget. It was not the result of a military brutality in a savage zone, but rather it was the legislated, authorised policy of a national government which decreed the mass execution of one section of the Revolution's quasi-divine entity, 'The People', after they had been re-defined as 'the scum of society'. The Convention declared that all Vendéens without exception were guilty. Carrier, speaking to the Comité and to the Convention on 11 December, gave legality to Turreau's task of genocide, stating that "the land had to be purged absolutely and totally."

This acceleration of extermination, from individuals, to groups, until it became a whole people in la Vendée must be recognised for what it was. It was the extreme and critical phase of democratic structuralism, helpless in its own crisis to stop itself.

The genocide began in Nantes with Carrier its revolutionary Pro-Consul. The guillotine was erected, Place du Bouffay. By mid-December the need to increase the number of executions became urgent as more and more had to be beheaded. Tumbrils soon rolled to the Square bearing young girls and children, some of whom had not even had judgment passed on them. Held up by their mothers, four young girls from General Charette's family were part of the sinister cortège. As the crowd saw them pass in the carts, so young, so beautiful, so dignified, they began to murmur their shock and disapproval. Carrier ordered the pavements of the square to be painted red to hide the blood. One by one the tumbrils emptied. One by one the heads fell. As the girls waited their turn they began to sing hymns. Among the crowd people began to weep. Ten days later the executioner died of shame. Soon the six cemeteries of the town were full. Mass graves were dug, with only a shovelful of earth between layers. In eight months they had registered twelve thousand burials.

The guillotine became inadequate to the Republican task. Carrier declared La Loire a Republican River – "A Revolutionary Torrent!" he exclaimed in his enthusiasm. From among the clergy imprisoned at Nantes for refusing to take the oath of the Civil Constitution, which effectively abolished catholic christianity, he chose the first ninety victims. It was 18 November, 1793.

The priests were bound and taken aboard 'La Gloire'. Holes were made along the sides of the barge, and it was sunk outside the harbour. It was ideal – sure, no noise, no witnesses, under cover of night. They could be tied up by the dozen, by the hundred. With ship sunk the operation was terminated. A prison could be emptied for its next customers. The method proved a success. Each boatload enthused its executioners more. "They were complaining in prison of hunger, at least they won't die of thirst." As in Soviet Russia, the State officials of genocide soon evolved their own macabre vocabulary of death. 'The Watering Place', 'the Chateau d'Eau', 'the Big Cup', 'the Patriotic Baptism'. Drowning – certainly not. It was 'déportation verticale', or even a 'Republican Marriage', now that the manner of execution had become to be tied together, naked, one against the other, man and woman, before sending them to the bottom of the sea.

That was the beginning. Then came General Turreau. In Paris they were openly declaring that the name Vendée had to be wiped out forever, renamed 'Vengé'. Barère, from the High Tribune of the Assembly, intoxicated, sang the Carmagnole with a refrain he sang out five times: "Destroy la Vendée." The Clubs, Jacobins leading, called out:

"Words. Words. History does not wait. To arms, citizens!"

The catalogue of actions began to be drawn up. Mobilisation against the Vendéen brigands. Expropriation of their goods. Clearance of their woods and forests. Seizure of their harvests and livestock, deportation of its population, women and children. Move in colonists. A Scientific Committee was set up to find newer and more efficient means of extermination. Sheep had been used in the experimental phase of the guillotine. Now sheep were to be used in trials of toxic gas. Half the sheep tested died of asphyxiation. Carrier was thrilled. Gas them. General Marcé was condemned and executed in September 1793, for lack of genocidal effectiveness and defeat at Chantonnay. Robespierre shouted: "In the combat of Liberty against Tyranny, it is necessary to make an example!" Danton called for three hundred thousand men to set out and destroy La Vendée.

After the battles of the Vendéen army from 17 October '93 to the last charge at Savenay, 23 December, a Republican captain Westermann sent a message to the Committee of Public Safety in Paris, "The Vendée is no more! It is dead beneath the sabre of Liberty, with its women and children.

I have just buried it in the marshes of Savenay. I have crushed its children under our horses' hoofs and massacred its women. You cannot accuse me of having taken prisoners."

When he entered the Convention he grasped the Tribune and declared: "I have exterminated the last 80,000 rebels!" Now it was the turn of Turreau, the final turn of the French genocide to move to its completion. A trap of fire and steel was laid across the Vendée from east to west, it was to leave nothing behind but ashes and corpses. Imperially this son of the Revolution informed 'the People', that is to say the Convention: "My intention is to burn everything. To eliminate the horde of brigands I regard it as indispensable to burn towns, villages, hamlets and farms. I need an express authorisation or a decree. Do we put all women and babies to the sword? You must decree this for me. With your authorisation and support within two weeks there will not be a horse or an inhabitant in La Vendée. La Vendée must be a national cemetery." Signed General Turreau, General-in-Chief, the Western Army.

So the People's Army marched, adorned with necklaces of human ears, the heads of babies and foetuses on their bayonets. At Nantes, in famine, they gathered pots of human fat from the crematory ovens of Bolage. At Pont-de-Cé a tannery specialised in the removal of skin tissue chosen from selected subjects by their surgeons, archetypal models for those democratic armies to come in settler America and Nazi Germany, as well as Communist Cambodia.

The Fifth Column under Cordelier surrounded a terrified village which took refuge in the Church. Voyneau, the local priest, flung himself in front of his flock asking they be saved. They cut out his tongue and his heart before cutting it in pieces. The next day one of the Resistance priests returned to find the whole village massacred in its streets and church. Before burying them he took down the inventory of the genocide: 564 people of whom 47 infants and babies. Amiand the contemporary Vendéen author asks: "1944 – Oradour-sur-Glane, Haute-Vienne? No! 1794 – Les Lucs-sur-Boulogne, Vendée."

General Huché halted his slaughter at Murtagne. They brought him two peasants, father and son. "Don't shoot them!" he cried. "Grease your bayonets on them." A little later the soldiers asked permission to finish them off by pistol: "They don't want to die." The General roared back, "Out of the question. By the sword – thrust it in, turn it, slash it!" Huché wrote to his superior, Turreau, on 17 February, "I have put to the sword the whole population of La Verrie, 500 of them, men and women." Turreau replied: "Courage my comrade. If every officer was killing as many as you, by the hundreds, we'd soon be finished."

To this bleak slaughter across a whole country have to be added the terrible statistics of drowned citizens, forced, gagged and bound onto boats which were then scuppered in mid-river, and with that undeniable misogynism of revolutionary passion came the still crueller practice of stripping a man and woman naked, binding them tightly face to face, before the ritual drowning. All this was watched with recorded pleasure.

The conclusion reached by Patrice Gueniffey simply went either un-noticed or not understood. It is a political assessment, not an historical one, and a judgment almost unthinkable to an atheist and rationalist society still sustained by an ethical discourse, even if that discourse in turn impinges on political realities. He stated: "It is true that the Revolution raised 'the People' to the rank of Divinity, but it celebrated the cult of an abstract people, part juridical principle – the sovereign people, part literary figure – the virtuous labourer and the honest artisan, which had little to do with real people."

In 1794 the Revolution passes from executions to genocide through its own inner logical process. It is the structuralist model of the executioner's axe. In the Vendée it does not only kill combatants taken prisoner and those suspected of having taken up arms to aid the insurrection. It kills the non-combatants of every age, the women like the men. 15 January 1794, Turreau insists that the Minister of War authorise "the outcome of the women and children." His order is to "empty the country within a fixed time." General Grignon insists it is not enough to kill the enemy but also "all those we believe to be our enemies." It is this same democratic logic that insists on Guantanamo and the secret execution camps of Afghanistan in the twenty-first century.

Gueniffey's recognition is of the truth that a people have to be destroyed *because they exist* as a 'rebel race', that is a *naturally* rebel people which the Republic, of its submissive nature, cannot assimilate. It is the Convention itself which defines the whole people of the Vendée as 'guilty'. Once legalised, the right to kill those who might rebel in future acts, the right to the execution of the children and the unborn, is granted.

Why give the grisly details of Republican slaughter? Two reasons: one – to remember that civic murder and massacre is always preceded by constitutionally sanctioned legislation which in turn is assured moral neutrality by the re-defining of its victims as non-persons, enemies of the people, along with de-humanising evaluations: terrorists, brigands, wild dogs, wolves. Two – another factor of democratic atrocities is that they are always met by the indifference of the 'democratic community'. What happens in La Vendée, in Concentration Camps be they in Republican America, German Reich, Soviet Russia, South Africa or Afghanistan – it is somehow unreal, unfortunate, and inevitable. The price we pay!

This forces on us the conclusion that the doctrine of humanism on which the current hegemony is founded contains within it, not outside it or despite it, a necessary rhetoric of de-humanisation, one which may be applied when the extermination of any recalcitrant group of humans becomes necessary or desirable.

In the looking-glass world of end-game politics,

by that term may be defined the final tottering propositions which modern super-structures need to justify now quite irrational policies, the only move left on the board for the 'democratic system' is to pre-empt exposure by the ultimate reversing of terms. Thus in contemporary language the enemies of the Super-State represent the Terror, i.e. are terrorists, thus the inchoate rebels are defined as the structured enemy, while the Super-State poses as the free-range open society of potential independence, although it is the Terror itself, Assembly, Congress, Parliament, all united in the original French model.

It follows from this that in the 'Terror' phase, which requires its genocide, in order to maintain the internal logic of the system, a dictator is necessary, but that dictator may only function within the Assembly system. Thus the dictator in a democracy functions with a parliamentary legitimisation. It is the fabrication of *enemies* which authorises the Terror of the State and the logical pulsation towards dictatorship.

In the unfolding of its inherent nature, the genocide which in turn requires a legitimated dictator leads to a new internal necessity. The humanist State requires a sanction for mass murder that cannot derive, or be seen to derive from humanism, for that would reveal its inescapable paradox. At this point the atheist power system is compelled to adopt a licensing theism. Such a theism cannot be 'natural' as that would contain the central doctrine of genuine religion, compassion. Thus a fabricated, man-made theism devoid of inner moral imperatives must be designed. Here is Gueniffey's analysis:

"Voted two days after the festival of the Supreme Being, the Law of 22 Prairial, Year II (of the post-christian calendar), that is 10 June, 1794, reformed the organisation and procedures of the Revolutionary Tribune of Paris, and inaugurated the Great Terror. From its installation on 6 April 1793 up to 10 June 1794, the Tribunal had judged 2,277 detainees, and pronounced 1,216 death sentences. In the seven weeks between the vote of the Law and the fall of Robespierre on 27 July it pronounced 1,784 sentences of which 1,409 were of capital punishment. The number of executions, less than a hundred a month during the first fourteen months of activity by the Revolutionary Tribunal, thus rose to around two hundred a week, that is to say nearly ten times more."

The necessity of the power system to claim

Divine authority when it moves into genocidal mode was clearly understood by Dostoevsky in his life's critique of modern nihilism. The doctrinal adoption of Evangelical religion, itself un-recognisable as historical christianity, was a categorical imperative for Bush before his genocidal sweep across the Iraqi valley and the mountains of Afghanistan. His English counter-part was also driven to linking his collaboration to his having received Divine sanction.

The Great Terror was not viewed as some kind of mal-function of the State or an abuse with a bureaucratic base, but precisely as an instrument for the elimination of the 'enemies of the People'.

Couthon flatly declared ('Moniteur'. vol. 20, p. 695): "It was not a question of making examples of some, but of either the extermination of the implacable satellites of Tyranny or our perishing along with the Republic."

Couthon traced the authority of the Law of 10 July 1794 back to the discoveries of Robespierre and Saint-Just on 13 November 1792. This indicated that the call for the execution of the King without a judgment was the pivotal, inseminating event of the foetus of the Terror.

Robespierre's demand was to negate the concept of the King's innocence. If found guilty it implied there was also a plea of innocence. To acquit the King was to condemn the People!

The Revolution, claimed Robespierre, does not punish, it obliterates. This was the meaning of Guantanamo, of the rendition of prisoners, stripped of nationality, name and identity, to torture and unrecorded death in remote satellite States.

Robespierre's 'idea' – the Republic – envisages a social order of Divine authority with one determined end, the blossoming of man as a moral being. To him man is created to practise morality. By the time he employs the term Republic in 1792 the doctrine of Liberty has become sophisticated. It is now constrained, as it was not in 1789, to submit its freedoms to respect the superior rule of justice. No longer can freedom licence withdrawal, selfishness or defiance of the social edict. The individual right of liberty must now conform to the needs of all.

On 24 April 1793 the Convention was presented with the project of the Declaration of the Rights of Man. Thus the Decree of 7 May 1794 recognising the existence of the Supreme

Being and the immortality of the soul and that of the Rights of Man found its political actualisation in the Great Terror. This, not by logical development but by the specific nature of one man – Robespierre. Gueniffey categorises unarguably the identity of Robespierre as the incarnation of the ideal bourgeois. The values of French society at the end of the 18th century were – work, family virtues, 'honest mediocrity', wealth, moderation of passions, and concern for the public good. In a wry footnote Gueniffey comments:

"Benjamin Franklin outlined the 13 moral virtues which defined the good life of the ideal bourgeois: temperance, silence, order, decisions, moderation, zeal, loyalty, equity, self-possession, propriety, moral balance, chastity and humility. Robespierre does not speak of anything else!"

At the core of Robespierre's position is that fundamental historicity which is the hallmark of the bourgeoisie. In theory universalist, in practice individualist, egotist. Robespierre's bedside bible was Rousseau's 'Social Contract' – but Rousseau is also the author of 'Reveries du Promeneur Solitaire'.

As François Furet noted: "The French Jacobins

of 1793 who are considered to be the ones who opened the rule of the bourgeoisie, nevertheless offer the first massive example of bourgeois who detest the bourgeois in the name of bourgeois principles." In other words this is the self-hatred which is to end in the 19th century with its logical conclusion – nihilism.

It is at this point that a certain recognition has to be granted, since failure to do so assures the repetition of the process which ends in Terror. What has to be recognised is that political processes, however structured and however internally logical, are dependent on an individual or individuals to set them up, set them in motion and ultimately to set them down. It could be said that the great failure of 20th century thinkers and indeed politicians was their inability to link the practice to the person, and then to analyse the person as actuator, not just as participant. There could have been neither Communism without Stalin, nor a bank without a banker.

The structuralist State which was the machine of Jacobinism, was in its turn the product of Saint-Just and Robespierre. The masses neither wanted nor recognised Jacobinism for what it was, but these two men placed all France under its orders, so that with both of them beheaded and the Terror over, the monstrous and inhuman machine lay waiting for a new driver, Napoleon, this time a genius who made of it the foundations of that archetypal State on which all subsequent States were to be based.

The present intellectual climate is one on which the clouds lower over the head of each monarch. We register his self-glorification, his bellicose ambitions, his cruelty, his favourites – all social and civic blame is heaped on his head. Now this is not completely wrong. What is disastrously wrong is what follows the creation of the structuralist States. No-one is, never mind to blame, ever responsible. No-one, apparently, is called to take responsibility for the mass carnage of World War I. Or rather, ironically, Princip's bullets fired at the Archduke Ferdinand and his consort, unleashed the combined fury of the great armies of Austria, Germany, France, Russia and Britain. Millions are driven off to the slaughter of the trenches – not one man responsible, and certainly not one man to say stop. Marshal Foch lamented that the age of Kings was over. Their wars saw far less casualties. The wars of the People saw the millions die. A King led his army. The politicians stayed at home. The ultimate irony lies in the ultimate democracy, America.

The President boasts that he is the Commander-in-Chief. In his business suit he even adopts a military salute. Yet he not once has ever seen active duty on the front line. The cowards send the brave to die. Again their claim of innocence is correct. They did not *do* it. The social framework did it. Presidents and Prime Ministers are front men. They are there to draw attention away from the active participants of the machine State. It is of the nature of the structuralist system that it should be autonomous and at the same time claim to be a leader-led willing coalition of free men. In other words, responsibility did not vanish with the assassination of the Kings. It became hidden, not conspiratorially hidden but structurally embedded in a series of interlinked systems that come together at key transversal power points – like the acupuncture grid of Chinese medicine. There, unelected, and often quite unknown to the masses, a small, decreasing oligarchic minority govern the destinies of the ignorant masses, nowhere more ignorant than in the high information technology zones of the world.

Fatally this intricate logical grid that is the Jacobin modern State, at the same time that it is impersonal and inhuman, seems of its very nature to provide a man of powerful will with an arena which he can take over, dominate, and lead to an apocalyptic end or a frenzied climax of genocide. Faced with 'discovery' by the Russian masses of the Stalinist Holocaust, which they had for decades placidly accepted, some kind of explanation was necessary. How did the scientifically designed State, based on its Marxist-Leninist Humanism, guided by the morally pure dictatorship of the Proletariat, end up a savage machine of mass-murder in the hands of a drunken and paranoid psychopath? The post-Stalinist regime in the Kremlin offered up the theory of the 'Cult of Personality'. Unfortunately, that is simply unacceptable as a thesis inside their system of dialectical materialism. It is an openly Hegelian idea which if admitted makes nonsense of the whole Soviet philosophical system. Sartre, not a little ashamed of his post-Marxist thinking, tried to help them out, to no avail.

The inevitable genocidal dictator seemed to be an inescapable part of a socially locked-in and rigidly structured State – the free radical with a will to destroy using the passive and helpless obedience of a people restricted to following orders to the end.

Do not avoid the implications of this analysis. The distinction that sets democracy against totalitarianism may have seemed convincing half a century ago – today it will not play! The massacres of the Israeli democracy, Viet Nam, Iraq, Afghanistan, the tortures, and the imprisonment without a trial even envisaged – all this is the now passively accepted face of democracy today.

In the Jacobin, that is modern democratic State, divergence of opinion is not just an error, it is a crime. As previously noted, in a debate in June 1791, Robespierre declared: "Whoever does not see the necessity of their dismissal is a fool. Whoever does see it and does not want it and does not propose it – is a traitor!" This is the inexorable logic of the democratic State when opposed in its absolute authority. Whoever is not with me is against me. Whoever is against me is the enemy of justice. Whoever is the enemy of justice is the enemy of the People. Now these are precisely the words of the American President at the beginning of the 21st century, and then as now these words are received by the elected representatives of the People with rapturous applause.

The democratic State transforms into its own dictatorship without any need for a Napoleonic intervention. Its own internal mechanisms can provide the means for a permanent coup d'état, and it will then as now be seen as 'the Patriot's Act'.

Robespierre was known as The Incorruptible. He saw his task as being to restore purity and abolish vice in France. He announced: "Considering to what a point the human species has been degraded by the vice of our former social system (the Ancien Régime), I am convinced of the necessity to carry out a complete regeneration, and if I may put it this way, to create a new People." This is the rhetoric of Stalin and his new Soviet Man, as it is of Nietzsche and his Übermensch, the phoenix vision of a renewed bourgeoisie.

The fabrication of an exalted, purifying and cleansing revolutionary hero can now be seen as the sordid construction of an actor on the political stage. The political leader, as such, is always thus. The mediocre little bourgeois non-entity emerges as a ritualised hero on the high kothurnus of his power to wield death and destruction, a great and tottering figure of Greek tragedy. Hitler, Lenin, Bush, Kemal, Blair, even little Bonaparte, all little men exalted by power, who scarcely knew the names of their own grandfathers. The theory of the Terror becomes the high rhetoric which licenses mass-murder in the name of social renewal and cleansing, yet its practice reveals it for what it is, a brutal power struggle. The heads of Danton, Desmoulins, and one by one all the other Committee men must fall in order that Robespierre should attain ultimate power. It is no accident that the climax of his political power should be marked by the inauguration of the festival dedicated to the Supreme Being over which he presided on June 8. On July 26 1794 he gave his last speech to the Convention.

"Let us say then that a conspiracy against public freedom exists: that it owes its force to a criminal coalition which is plotting inside the Convention itself: that this coalition has conspirators in the Committee of General Security, and in the offices of this Committee they are dominant: that the energies of the Republic have set this Committee against the Committee of Public Safety, thus constituting two governments: that some members of the Committee of Public Safety have entered into this plot: that the resulting coalition thus formed seeks an end to both Patriots and Motherland.

"What is the remedy for this sickness? Punish the traitors, renew the offices of the Committee of General Security, purge this Committee itself, and make it subordinate to the Committee of Public Safety. Purge the Committee of Public Safety itself, in order to constitute the unity of government under the supreme authority of the National Convention, which is the centre and the judge, and so crush all the serious factions of national authority, in order to raise up on their ruins the power of justice and freedom."

Robespierre had created his own Divine Supreme Being. Now he took his place unequivocally as the sole interpreter of its Divine Will, but the Terror was not defeated by the opponents of Terror, but by the other terrorists who wanted to take over the pending renovation of the Government to their advantage. However, if the Incorruptible fell there could not be another one. The death of Robespierre at that very point when he made his bid for absolute dictatorship marked the end of an epoch. Michelet claimed it marked the end of the French Revolution. It means the end of the effort to submit the nation to a cleansing eschatological fire so that it could emerge cleansed and peopled by New Men. What was left in its wake was the new structuralist State, atheist yet with a shadow Divinity to be invoked (or evoked) at days of commemoration, mourning, and before and after battle, secularist yet mystical. Government was now enmeshed inside its Constitutional grid, sustained by a spider's web of ministries, committees and spokesmen. No-one, that is to say, no longer one man was to be responsible for all the acts of power.

The old regime had a three-tiered structure:
1) The King and the Nobles
2) The Clergy
3) The Third Estate: the masses

The new regime had left in place:
1) The Assembly-Government
2) Empty
3) The enfranchised Citizens: the masses

The Clergy had over time evolved, via Richelieu and Mazarin, into the Financial Class. In the next stage of the Revolution as worked out by the successful dictator, Napoleon, the second estate emerged as the new religious group (Proudhon, remember, called them the Sect), the Financiers. Napoleon created La Banque de France, and a new upper class began to emerge, later dominating both government and masses. Its instrument of power was the new abstract money, without collateral, the paper 'Assignats' on which the modern world was to be founded. By it the Citizens of the 'Demo-cracy' – that system which lay in the ruins of the Revolution – were to be transformed into Debtors.

Since Robespierre emerged from being just another Revolutionary, to be that pivotal figure who cast his dark shadow over the Revolution and brought about its fall, he cannot be passed over as an attendant knight – he was its Hamlet and its Prince. It is here that can be discovered what was the reality which lay hidden under the Revolution's exalted rhetoric and its sordid genocide. In this man can be found the identity of that social convulsion which ends with the total enslavement of mankind, political democracy, rather, in two men, Robespierre and Saint-Just.

III

With the arrival of the bourgeois Robespierre on the stage of history the age of government by lawyers can be dated. Born in 1758 he was to be guillotined in 1794, an event which, while it did not end the Great Terror, led to the slaughter of the counter-Terror which did end it, leaving its Jacobin ideology to be restored by the dictator Napoleon.

After Robespierre's mother's death his father abandoned his children and took off for Germany, leaving the young Maximilien as head of the house. So it is that before considering his political career the inevitable consequences of his desolate childhood must be recognised. To the child who loses its mother early, that departure is known to be seen in many cases not as a tragedy but as a betraying, an abandonment, as if chosen to punish a wicked offspring. In the same way the desertion of the father is openly offensive, one might say in family terms, political. The former merits a judicial punishment, but the latter could indicate a revenge, a perhaps never confronted or known revenge but that one day had to be acted out.

His concern for the poor earned him the name of the Incorruptible, but as noted earlier he nursed an aspiration to belong to the nobility, even to the extent of ennobling his own name. He 'believed' in the abolition of the death penalty yet was to be the first author of genocide in the heartland of European civilisation.

Guglielmo Ferrero in his study on power noted that as the Terror became a reality which every day became more horrible it needed to be held against an ever more elevated ideal. He said: "The Jacobins did not shed so much blood because they believed in the sovereignty of the People as a religious truth, but rather, they were forced to believe in the sovereignty of the People as a religious truth, because their fear had made them shed so much blood." He goes further stating a devastating conclusion, one which the democratic sons of the Revolution simply cannot confront: "It was fear and the need for the absolute which led the Revolution to make the 'Social Contract' its Bible and Rousseau its Moses."

A far from original politique and psychology can be discerned in Robespierre. It is that of the ascetic, virginal monk of medieval christianity whose reforming zeal to raise people up from paganism muddily mixed with the repression resulting from celibacy led inescapably to torture and burning of witches and the full horror of the Inquisition, that primal model of legalism fronting mass slaughter. Shunning the vice of pagan Rome they dreamed of creating a 'new man in Christ' who would arise from the cleansing bath of baptism.

In the light of this, read Robespierre's political statement and recognise its metaphysical pretension: "And considering to what a point the human species has been degraded by the vice of our former ('ancien') social system, I am convinced of the necessity to carry out a complete regeneration and, if I may put it this way, to create a new people."

This is the Enlightenment version of the christian declaration: "Behold, I make all things new!"

Everything in the 'Alltäglichkeit' of Robespierre was disturbing, but the political class are notorious for failing, such is their belief in policy and structures, to recognise the clear outward signs of serious flaws in the make-up of a man.

Danton, the fellow Revolutionary, who set up the structural system which destroyed them both, looked on Robespierre as a friend, but as an ideological friend, dedicated like him to the murder of the Royal Family. Yet lurking underneath is Robespierre's hidden loathing of the hedonism and womanising which set Danton apart from his friend. More murky still, Robespierre's closer friend Camille Desmoulins stands out in conflict with him not only because he proposes moderation, freedom of speech and debate – but because when the avenging moment comes it is not only Camille who must be guillotined but also his lovely and loving wife, Lucille. Robespierre was to tell the Committee that they had betrayed the Revolution by making secret contracts with the enemy, but, in deep, the contract that his vengeful fury fell upon was that which Danton had made with his many women, and worse, Camille's contract with his loving wife, Lucille.

Modern democracy, historically obliged to admit it is the child of the Revolution and the Terror, has felt obliged to raise up Danton as its 'true' founder – moderate, restrained and a genuine 'Enlightenment' hero. Indeed, today he is thus displayed, so that we are obliged to look up to his heroic statue as it gazes beyond us in eternal Olympic contemplation from its exalted plinth at the Place de l'Odeon in Paris. In the 'official' bi-centenary comprehensive study 'L'État de la France' it begins his biography with a denial that he was ugly! Indeed it places the word 'laideur' in inverted commas, giving his falsely attributed ugliness mythic status. It is, they tell us, a legend "transmitted in hundreds of books on the Revolution". Now, Danton was not ugly, they tell us. He was "broad-shouldered and of great physical force – only he still bore on his face the results of a blow from a horse's hoof or from a bull which had scarred his jaw in infancy. He was attractive when he wanted to be, and he often wanted to be," glows the Revolutionary version.

The great political theorist Hilaire Belloc in his sympathetic biography, 'Danton', said: "He was tall and stout. ... His upper lip was injured, and so was his nose, and he had further been disfigured by the smallpox. His lip had been torn by a bull as a child, and his nose crushed in a second adventure, they say, with the same animal." The 'official' 'État de la France' does not mention his smallpox yet it does not fail to inform us that the pro-monarchist De Mirabeau had "an over-enlarged head and a face marked in childhood by smallpox."

The reality obscured by this hagiography is more serious that the matter of his face – although the good-looking Danton according to them showed his defiance and insouciance on the scaffold when he called to the executioner, "You must show my head to the people. It looks good!" – it is surely nobler than that – it was his final ironic reconciliation with his own ugliness. The character of Danton takes its value from being the acceptable face of the Revolution and its Terror. Now, officially beautiful, but in truth ugly but lit with an ardour to rescue mankind. Without Danton none of it could have happened. He was the archetypal politician, emotional orator and clinical organiser. He was the structuralist genius of the lawyer-élite based society which now functions from the USA to Britain, France and Germany. Had there been doubt of this his end remains to prove it. He it was who structurally set up the Revolutionary tribunal that was to execute him, his fellow 'moderates' and finally his 'extremist' enemies.

Alexandre Dumas ends his book on the Revolution in his 'Histoire de France' with another encounter at the guillotine. As the three friends were bound at the scaffold, hands behind the back, Dumas' hero declares: "It is the done thing to call out 'Long Live' something or other when you die. Once upon a time they used to cry 'Long Live the King!' But there is no more King. After that they cried, 'Long Live Liberty!' But there is no more liberty. Why not 'Long Live the Revolutionary,' who had joined all three of us victims together."

Suppose for a moment that Danton could be granted amnesty from the Dumasian view that the Revolutionaries must bear responsibility collectively for their enormous crimes. Still a question remains: how did Danton not see who Robespierre was, or Saint-Just, or Carnot, or Marat? Was it perhaps that political structuration and programmation blinded men to men, to their inner structuration, to their hidden programmation?

Bukharin, who fervently believed in the socialist Revolution up to his execution, went to his death just because he simply could not 'see' who Stalin was. The shared life of struggle, the mutual sacrifices, the political collaboration, the long friendship, none of these mattered when Bukharin emerged as a negating factor of the irrepressible dialectic. It was as if the Revolution in its inexorable working-out was justified in requiring the life of Bukharin. But legal structures do not execute people. In every case people kill people. Stalin killed Bukharin, but Bukharin never seems to have grasped that the flaw in the political system that he had espoused was that it required Stalin to kill and Bukharin to be killed – along with twenty million more. Tocqueville saw the crack in the machine. He said in his 'Consideration sur la Revolution' (Pleiade II, p.492): "The concept of government becomes simple: number itself makes the law and the rights. All of politics is reduced to a question of arithmetic."

Firstly, let us look at Robespierre and Saint-Just as they may be viewed both in their policies and the tenor of their pronouncements. Secondly, let us look at what manner of men they were, for this is a matter that has been viewed by the democratic upholders of their foundational institution, the

Revolution, with an abnormal reticence and prudishness. That we are obliged to examine them together is part of the story, and our concern.

Robespierre declared: "The Republic unites us against all vicious men. ... One rules the People by reason and its enemies by Terror. The Government of the Republic is the despotism of liberty against tyranny. Whoever does not hate crime is incapable of loving virtue."

Saint-Just declared: "Monarchy is not a question of kingship, it is a crime. The Republic is not a question of Senate, it is a virtue."

Robespierre in a speech of 5 February 1794 said: "In our country, we want to replace egoism with morality, honour with honesty, the tyranny of fashion with the rule of reason, contempt for misfortune with contempt for vice, insolence with self-respect, vanity with greatness of soul, love of money with love of 'gloire', good company with good people, intrigue with merit, wit with genius, show with truth, the tediousness of dissipation with uncloyed happiness, the pettiness of 'les Grands' with the greatness of man, an amiable, frivolous and wretched people with one that is magnanimous, strong and happy, that is to say all the vices and stupidities of the monarchy with all the virtues and miracles of the Republic. (Applause)."

Saint-Just, 10 October 1793: "You have no more grounds for restraint against the enemies of the New Order, and liberty must prevail at any price. ... You must punish not merely traitors but the indifferent as well – you must punish whoever is passive in the Republic. ... These maxims, peace and justice, hold good as between friends of liberty, but between the People and its enemies there is only the sword in common. We must rule by iron those who cannot be ruled by justice. ... The Constitution cannot be implemented – people would use it to destroy it. It would protect attempts against liberty, because it would lack the force necessary to repress them."

Report from the 'Bureau de Police': A clerk of the former Parlement has said, "The present order of things cannot last." Robespierre's directive: Find the address of the delinquent and have him arrested.

Saint-Just: "The duty of the legislator is to transform people into what he wants them to be."

Their close Revolutionary comrade, Barère, defined the correct position thus: "True humanity consists of exterminating one's enemies." Saint-Just confirmed this, stating: "What constitutes a Republic is the complete destruction of what is opposed to it. In a Republic, which can only be based on virtue, any pity shown towards crime is a flagrant proof of treason."

The pro-Revolutionary discourse, one taught and disseminated by state school systems and the monolithic university system whose doctorate of philosophy imposes a world-wide methodology of critical analysis, has in effect ended up with a kind of consensus on the Revolution. The Terror was necessary and inescapable, but a price worth paying. It was equivalent to the birth-pangs of a mother – worth the trouble – the prelude to the emergence of the child, liberal democracy. In order to achieve this cool detachment which permits the cross-over from personal rule to constitutional rule it has proved necessary to step back from individuals who participated in this massive social convulsion. Yet it could scarcely be convincing that such a trans-valuation had been accomplished by ordinary folk motivated by a modest reformist zeal. It has proved necessary to prevent a close-up study of the characters in the drama. They have to be, in short, de-personalised. They are, in the current world-view, masked with indicative masks that tell us at a glance not their 'who' but their 'what'. As has been noted, this has permitted a larger than life statue of Danton to be set up on the Place de l'Odeon. It has permitted the renaming of the place of the execution of France's King as 'Place de la Concorde'. It has even respectfully set Robespierre's shaving mug in the Museum of Paris.

Mirabeau is psychologised, libidinous, corrupt – a syphilitic womaniser. Why does he merit this? Because he was humanly captivated by both the beauty and the predicament of the Queen. As a Revolutionary who 'crossed over' to the Royal Cause he became a fit subject for the psychological technique of de-construction.

Even Marat has to be viewed through the distant lens of ideology and party position, a vital icon of the Revolution's dialectic. Charlotte Corday, his assassin, has to submit to the distorting lens of close-up subjective appraisal blurred in turn by a doctrinal misogynism.

The two central actors on the stage of the Terror have been definitively set up as the dual icons of

Revolutionary dynamism, single-mindedness and majesty. Midwives, not dismayed by the bloodiness of birth, even glamorous in their fastidious detachment. They were the key players in the drama. The aristocracy were torn from power and guillotined en masse. In their place a new class seized both power and system, replacing aristocracy came the lawyers. They are certainly the patriarchs of the new ruling élite as is proven today in both the EU and the USA where lawyer Presidents and Prime Ministers are the rule not the exception.

Christianity, by their hands, was abolished. The clergy which had, certainly since Richelieu, been the financial class, were swept aside and massacred enthusiastically. In their place came a new financial élite with a new currency. The bankers, who had been slowly gaining power since Louis XIV, emerged with a new evaluation of money. In place of the dyad, gold and silver coin embossed with the monarch's head, came a new currency, paper money. In place of intrinsic 'real' wealth – gold, came the new wealth, worth in real terms only the paper it was printed on – in practice valued by the numbers on it, workable, yet doomed to fluctuation and inflation depending on what backed it up. One day it would break free of the ties of collateral and remain an abstract numerical system disappearing even from its paper form to be the world tyrannising web of a wealth system itself reduced to flashing electronic signals of information passing between computer terminals.

One could say that the guillotining of Louis XVI was the political event which in itself was symbolic, Danton understood this, while its reality was that when his bloody head fell into the basket, at the same time it was removed from the Golden Louis, and with the King went the gold. Paper money issued by bankers was the new Régime. All this needed a very special sacrificial priesthood, and the two High Priests were unquestionably that odd couple, Robespierre and Saint-Just. The Revolution's two heroes were chaste and they were pure, but is that natural – were they natural?

With the historical record in its now official version, what is discovered is that an unusual 'pudeur' has covered up the narrative. Just as Danton is transformed into an alluring figure, Mirabeau into a pockmarked dissolute, and while the King is presented as a bumbling and uninformed fool – with the two Revolutionaries at the heart of regicide and genocide the record presents a fastidious puritan idealist, the 'Incorruptible', and the cool aloof beauty of someone described as an angel! It is as if the last century had not constructed a very clear analytical system of varied psychological means to look at what Jane Arden, the renowned English feminist, referred to as 'the other side of the underneath'. Robespierre and Saint-Just – chaste and pure, the primal celibate couple of Terror – is that the whole story – the immaculate and the angel?

Saint-Just was deeply involved in the creation of Republican institutions which would define and govern child education. "Young children should not be struck and should not be caressed." He was also concerned to legislate the limits and nature of male friendship.

Saint-Just had a utopian dream of a world, virile and virginal, in which women played no role. In his view of the world they did not exist. To him the world consisted of 'friends' who, without touching or speaking, would signal their mutual faithfulness. He wrote: "The friends are set one next to the other in combat. Those who have stayed united all their lives are buried in the same tomb. The friends wear mourning one for the other. The friends dig the grave, prepare the funeral one for the other. They may plant flowers at the sepulchre together with the children." (Saint-

Just: Institutions Républicanes, Oeuvres, p. 306).

As has already been observed, Robespierre preserved an ice-cold indifference to those deemed 'Enemies of the People', and his only intense emotional resistance to an execution was when Camille Desmoulins defied his political programme. He tried desperately to win him back, but once Desmoulins refused he took a ferocious revenge, killing both Desmoulins and his wife.

If that was the passionate attachment of Robespierre, Saint-Just on his side also had a passionate life-and-death 'friend'. When Saint-Just was arrested his friend Lebas insisted on being arrested along with him so that they could die together. As if even that suggested merely a political loyalty, Lebas at the last minute committed suicide as if to personalise his sacrifice.

Both Robespierre and Saint-Just believed that the child should be removed as soon as possible from the 'dangerous influence of the mother and the family'. In the most profound way, not philosophically but psychically and even, as shall be shown, mythically, Sparta not Athens conducted and orchestrated the great liberation theology of humanism. This deeply bonded couple require the elimination, indeed the murder, of the royal couple to legitimise their Revolutionary contract. Of all the great writers who have meditated on the events of the Revolution and the Terror, only Carlyle grasped the actual tenor or texture of what happened. He saw that in it there was a tempo and atmosphere of intensity, a rushing of events, a hurtling from one day to the next. An urgency, a frenzy fired by quotidian crises. In it all, capping its anti-rational atmosphere, a frothing foam of talk, speeches, curses, imprecations, slogans – the renowned rhetoric of the Revolutionary discourse.

At the trial of the King, Danton shouts out: "I am no politician! I vote for death." Saint-Just rushes forward to put his name to the death-sentence with a theatricality that unleashes in the Assembly its regicidal passion. Robespierre rambles on about his own incorruptibility: "I remain compassionate for the oppressed. I know nothing of that humanity which is forever sacrificing whole peoples and protecting tyrants. I vote for death."

At the trial of the Queen, when Hébert's outrageous accusation of incest almost sways the crowd in her favour – "I appeal to you as a mother!" – Robespierre is brought news of the prosecution's blunder and in his anger smashes a plate to the floor.

At the very heart of the affair, of the chaste revolutionary lovers, of the intense Revolutionary leadership, Marat, Danton, Hébert, Fouquier-Tinville, of the Girondins and the Montagnards, the Jacobins, deeper than regicide, is to be found the dark force of misogynism.

The poison and rage of hatred against womankind becomes over the years preceding the crisis of Revolution the ethos itself in which a transvaluation of values takes place. That ethical misogynism was to find its focus in the long series of attacks by Pamphlets on the Queen. Throughout her reign she had been the subject of scurrilous Pamphlets, the savagery of which went well beyond satire, and which caused anxiety to the Queen's mother, Marie-Thérèse, in Vienna. Significantly it was when the Queen became pregnant in 1778 that the Revolutionaries began their most ferocious attacks on her, their language, imagery and scenarios taking on a quite mythical character. Over years she was to be castigated in libellous documents which purported to demonstrate that she was a traitor, an adulteress, a sodomite, a lesbian, and a blood-drinking whore guilty of incest and infanticide.

The Republic in later years made sure that this literature of slander and pornography was destroyed so that it is impossible today to find it in antiquarian bookshops, except on rare occasions. However, there is still an ample historical evidence from many published excerpts and from private collections of what was once a massive literature, that literature being one of the vital motor-forces of a far from spontaneous civic uprising.

By 1789 the tone of the Pamphlets has passed from mockery to condemnation. Madame de Staël noted: "No-one differs more from the reputation that her enemies have tried to give her than the Queen. They have not even tried to make a resemblance in the lie, so much have they counted on that envy which knows exactly how to respond to the slanderers."

In the Pamphlets Marie-Antoinette is a pervert, a libertine whose sex is on fire for pleasure. She is a witch, a vampire, the wicked Queen of the fairy stories. She threatens not only the health of the citizens, and the finances of the country, but also the equilibrium of the world itself. The Pamphlets sometimes have her confessing in the first person, boasting rather, of her vices. "At the mere sight of a handsome man or a beautiful woman, my eyes blaze, my body comes to life, my orgasm takes over. Only with difficulty can I hide the violence of my desires." The women of her court are described as her bacchantes, the Trianon is her brothel.

The libels present a triumphant feminine orgasm, unbearable to masculine pride. The orgiastic Queen, the Tyrant, is the leader of the dance. "The nobility, the clergy, the peasants, every man has the right to her favours. The most handsome and the most robust are the most welcome." In the fantasy the Pamphlets weave, the Queen loves women. She exhausts the men without loving them while in reality she desires only her own sex. Her lesbianism the Pamphlets trace to her Austrian mother. She is the pupil of 'the School of Dangerous Women' which pervade Europe. At the time Marie-Antoinette arrived in Paris in 1770, Russia was ruled by Catherine II and Austria by Marie-Thérèse, with her crowning Europe was to be controlled by three powerful women. The fantasy of a lesbian plot covered men's fear that they had lost the upper hand in the government of the world.

The Queen's closest ladies in waiting were the object of virulent hatred. Mme. de Polignac was loathed as much as the Queen, even more when, fleeing to Rome, she escaped Revolutionary punishment. The Princess de Lamballe was not so fortunate. After being guillotined they cut off her sex and a horrified Mercier recorded that then one man amused himself by making a moustache of it. The Queen was transformed into a female monster to take her place alongside Messalina, Frédégonde and Medea. She was described as a ferocious animal of the jungle, she was a panther, an arch-tigress, a venomous snake. She bathed in her victims' blood. She declared, or rather her mythic self in the vast Pamphlet output, "My one desire is to see this capital city swimming in its own blood. Each French head offered up for me to see, I will pay its weight in gold."

A 1790 Pamphlet accuses her in its title: 'The Cause of the French Revolution or the Secret Conduct of Marie-Antoinette of Austria, Queen of France'. Chantal Thomas in her definitive study, 'The Wicked Queen: Marie-Antoinette in the Pamphlets' states categorically: "The simplistic idea of a country ruined by the expenses of a woman is clearly a pure fantasy. It is not the height of the coiffures, nor the golden robes, nor the shoes with diamond buckles, which can bring down a State. On the scene of historical events, Queens and their favourites, however fascinating they may be, can never be other than attendant players."

The official version of the cause of the Revolution, according to the Pamphleteers, and therefore in fact beyond their noms de plume the Revolutionaries themselves, was Marie-Antoinette. In the present day discourse it still is. Chantal Thomas in the Introduction to her masterly study gives a contemporary image which confirms that the Revolutionary lie is now the quotidian reality. "At the Carnavalet Museum a small boy asks his mother if Marie-Antoinette had been guillotined. 'Well done!' he adds."

In 1789 Camille Desmoulins tried ineffectively to pull back the surge of anti-feminine fury that was taking possession of the Revolutionary programme and discourse. He and his wife represent a kind of archetypal couple, the humane liberal team inside the radical camp who at a given moment try to halt the rush to murder, vengeance and the smashing of values that is the inescapable nature of the emergent State power. His tactic was to try and rescue the Queen from her calumniators by de-constructing her role in the political drama. If he could de-Queen her she might be saved. It was a futile but most significant ploy.

He wrote: "Two words which should astonish us if they appear together are 'Queen of the French'. The French do not have a Queen. Salic Law is formal. Marie-Antoinette of Austria is the wife of the King and nothing more. I believe this term is a matter of style, as one writes 'your servant' at the foot of a letter. But it is with words that one governs men." He goes on to make a distinction between the legislative power and the generative power. His proposal that calling her the Queen will somehow rescue her indicated his naïve failure to see that the Revolutionary project on which he and his wife had embarked was there precisely to abolish the politicality of the generative power. Marie-Antoinette had to be sacrificed to the new power of the male lawyer class, to the new logical system of structuralist State and its abstract money.

The legalist and absolutist State, the political democracy, spawned by the Revolution had no place in it for 'woman', already she had been subsumed under the term 'citizen', as such she was unsexed and deposed. The trial and execution of the Queen was the end of man's long vulnerability, helplessness, dependence and even domination by women. Now the rules were to rule. Rhetoric, that terrible male weapon, was to silence once and for all that unlicensed gaiety and delight and pleasure that was womanhood.

The actress, Rose Lacombe, had set up a women's movement, a first female attempt to break into the new sexless system. It was called 'Les Républicaines Révolutionaires'. It was banned on 30 October 1793. Amar declared: "Women are scarcely capable of high speculation and serious reflection. A woman should not leave her family to get involved in affairs of government." Again the false dialectic of Desmoulins can be observed. Of course, if that *is* the dialectic it is unjust and its synthesis can only end with the de-womanising of woman to reach a new 'citizen' type devoid of womanism, a hybrid who can 'fit in' to the structuralist archetype demanded of the new system. Just over two hundred years later the political democracy of Germany elected its first woman Chancellor, to do so she felt compelled – and was instructed by her media advisers – to enter the Bundestag as a transvestite, hair cropped and suit tailored.

The trial of the Queen is in every way as appalling as the execution of the Queen. Chantal Thomas defined it thus: "When the time for the Queen's trial came, the passions aroused by the images of the Infernal Woman had for far too long gone beyond the limits of credibility to be calmed. The incantatory delirium of the Pamphlets, the poetic eloquence of the saga of the Queen of Evil, continued to be active across the formulae of the interrogation and its dry succession of questions and answers."

In Chantal Thomas' analysis there is a dual energy operating. On the one hand she observes that the judgment, condemnation and execution unfold as punishment of the Queen's diabolical perversity and insatiable sexual voracity. On the other hand the word 'Queen' is forbidden. Before the justice of the People stands the widow Capet. Louis XVI was tried by the Convention – it was a political show trial, modelled deliberately on that of Charles I of Britain. Marie-Antoinette was brought before the Revolutionary Tribunal like any other 'accused' citizen.

The President of the Tribunal declared: "A woman who was surrounded by all the marks of the most brilliant prestige that the pride of kings and the baseness of slaves were able to invent, today stands before the tribunal of the nation, a place that was occupied two days ago by another woman, and this equality guarantees her impartial justice."

The 'impartial' trial, loaded with the vocabulary and images of the Pamphlets, replete with its shameless invention of the charge of incest against the Queen and her son, started on 14 October at eight in the morning and ended the next day at four-thirty. The jury, having met in closed session, at dawn, declared Marie-Antoinette guilty on all counts. She was called 'Antoinette' for she had been stripped not only of her rank but of her name. It was to the Revolutionary men unthinkable that she should bear the name of Marie, Mother of Jesus. The same un-naming had been imposed on Marie-Anne-Charlotte Corday, the 'monster' who had murdered the demented Marat. She was denounced as: "A virago, flabby, graceless, unclean as are all the clever philo-sophical females." The removal of the sacred name indicated to the jury that the accused was destined for the guillotine. Antoinette was to be guillotined for being foolish as Charlotte had been for being clever.

Munro Price in his important study 'The Fall of the French Monarchy' notes how just before the trial, the Queen had been moved from the Temple to the Conciergerie Prison next to the Palace of Justice on the Île de la Cité on 2 August. "The lack of warning, the hurried departure, the transfer in darkness; all bear the trademarks of the modern police state. The implication of the action was obvious. The Conciergerie was for prisoners about to be condemned, the 'antechamber of death'. ... She was put in a cell eleven and a half feet square, which she had to share with one female servant and two gendarmes." Later she was placed in solitary confinement.

Her health collapsed. She had lost a great deal of weight. Her hair was now white. Her eyesight had weakened. Her period pains were accompanied by excessive bleeding. At 6 pm on 12 October she was summoned before the Tribunal for a first examination. "Everything was designed to break her spirit," continues Price. "It was known that her period pains had begun and were particularly severe, and again the hours of darkness had been chosen for the ordeal. ... The only light came from two flickering candles." The trial was set for 14 October. The following day came the sentence. It was to be carried out in twenty-four hours.

She was forbidden to go to her death in mourning black, to avoid any risk of sympathy, so she went to the scaffold in white, with black stockings and a pair of elegant black silk shoes, last vestige of her vanished past.

The capital was put on a war footing. Cannons were set up across Paris, and troops moved about the city. The Place de la Révolution was seething with people. The mood was festive. The crowd ate, drank, and recited the Pamphlets aloud to raucous laughter. They listened, intensely, gasping, to: 'The Farewell of the Queen to her Lover-Boys and Girls', 'The Great Sickness of Marie-Antoinette', 'The Testament of the Widow Capet'.

At eleven o'clock on the morning of 16 October she was led out into the courtyard of the Conciergerie. Price described it: "Awaiting her there was the final barbarity; not a closed carriage that would permit her to die with decency like her husband, but the open tumbril reserved for common criminals. The Queen's composure momentarily deserted her at the sight, and she hastily had to relieve herself by the wall. The lapse was quickly over. The Queen climbed into the cart, her hands tied behind her back, and set off on her last journey. The cart took one hour to trundle the short distance from the Conciergerie to the Place de la Révolution. Marie-Antoinette did not blink under the jeering and cries of hatred which followed her progress. She descended from the tumbril lightly, and on the scaffold assisted the Executioner in his task."

The abominable Hébert saw it the democratic way: 'The bitch, added to that, was audacious and insolent up to the last.'

It was, and is recorded as, the end of the Ancien Régime. The end of monarchic tyranny. It was that, of course. At the same time it was much, much more. As a result, millions and millions have perished and continue to be eliminated by the new society. It was never to be Liberty. It was never to be Fraternity. It was never to be Equality. Now, only now can we begin to recognise what it was. It was the beginning of the Great Interregnum.

PART 2

I

Balzac wrote: "There are two histories, the official history, which is untrue and which is taught: then the secret history, where the causes of history lie, a shameful history..."

Dickens wrote: "Now, what I want is, Facts. Teach these boys and girls nothing but facts. Facts alone are wanted in life. Plant nothing else, and root out everything else. You can only form the minds of reasoning animals on facts: nothing else will ever be of any service to them. This is the principle on which I bring up my own children, and this is the principle on which I bring up these children. Sticks to Facts, Sir!"

With these words of the school-owner Mr Gradgrind, Dickens opened one of his final masterpieces, 'Hard Times'. It was never his intention to posit something so naïve as a world in which fancy stood apart from fact, leaving one still with a dichotomy of reality hard and brutal and illusion, soft and therapeutic. He was equally aware of the bitter facts of poverty in England all around him. What he had perceived was that the contradictions in society, that is its gross injustices, were perpetually sustained, licensed and pardoned by the imposition of a world-view which, basing itself on its facts, could utterly obliterate the compassionate evaluation of life, that is, lives themselves. The pupil, Sissy, explains to Louisa, the daughter of Mr Gradgrind, that the teacher had been explaining National Prosperity. She firstly misunderstands him, thinking he has said Natural Prosperity, and on being corrected asks if they are not the same thing.

"And he said, 'Now, this schoolroom is a Nation. And in this nation there are fifty millions of money. Isn't this a prosperous nation? Girl number twenty, isn't this a prosperous nation, and aren't you in a thriving state?'

'What did you say?' asked Louisa.

'Miss Louisa, I said I didn't know. I thought I

couldn't know whether it was a prosperous nation or not, or whether I was in a thriving state or not, unless I knew who had got the money, and whether any of it was mine. But that had nothing to do with it. It was not in the figures at all,' said Sissy, wiping her eyes.

'That was a great mistake of yours,' observed Louisa.

'Yes, Miss Louisa, I know it was, now. ... He said he would try me again. And he said, "This schoolroom is an immense town, and in it there are a million of inhabitants, and only five-and-twenty are starved to death in the streets, in the course of a year. What is your remark on that proportion?" And my remark was – for I couldn't think of a better one – that I thought it must be just as hard upon those who were starved, whether the others were a million, or a million million. And that was wrong, too!'

'Of course it was.'"

Dickens prefaced 'Hard Times' with a dedication, 'Inscribed to Thomas Carlyle'. Despite the famous two cartloads of books which Carlyle sent to Dickens from the London Library to help him research 'A Tale of Two Cities' he ended up with a narration of the Revolution as an event of intense barbarity which had, nevertheless, embedded in it an equally intense story of love which was to end with its protagonist on the scaffold in an act of both sacrifice and rescue. Significantly, Alexander Dumas in his epic history of France climaxes the Terror with his lovers going to the guillotine, united by love, beheaded by the State.

Carlyle, in 'Past and Present', explained:

"To predict the Future, to manage the Present, would not be so impossible, had not the Past been so sacrilegiously mis-handled: effaced, and what is worse, defaced! The Past cannot be seen; the Past, looked at through the medium of 'Philosophical History' in these times, cannot even be NOT seen: it is mis-seen. ... All was inane discord in the Past; brute force bore rule everywhere; Stupidity, savage Un-reason, fitter for Bedlam than for a Human World! ... The Dryasdust Philosophisms and enlightened Scepticisms of the Eighteenth Century, historical and others, will have to survive for a while with the Physiologists, as a memorable *Nightmare-Dream*. All this haggard epoch, with its ghastly Doctrines, and death's head Philosophies 'teaching by example' or otherwise, will one day have become, what to our Muslim friends their godless ages are, 'The Period of Ignorance'."

Once the false dialectic is rejected it becomes necessary to posit a new dynamic model both of perception and evaluation which may open a vision of hope and action for the future. The false dialectic is in thesis that the past was brutal, tyrannical and enslaving. The antithesis was that men heroically rose up and overthrew the 'Ancien Régime' of monarchy and privilege. The synthesis was that men in a system called democracy chose their own leaders by franchise, and in an un-voted codicil, that government had to be divorced from 'market forces' in order to function free of interference. It is this outrageous deception that has dominated men's thinking and action for over two hundred years and so disturbed great writers and so bamboozled the urban masses in the face of a world-wide carnage caused by war and poverty. The rejection of this dialectic, therefore, must in turn expose to daylight the still unquestioned codicil, the world-enslaving codicil.

Following the end of the age of personal rule it was assumed that one knew where the wealth had gone. It was assumed that it had been in the gift of kings. The official histories declared that wealth passed to government, that is to the National State ruled by its elected Senate or Parliament. Banking itself was assumed to be under State governance.

There was the Bank of England, then Napoleon himself created the Bank of France, then the archetypal political democracy, America, was finally to appoint a Federal Reserve Board. However, just as government had to be re-designed from a ruler surrounded by an advisory and inhibiting set of influential groupings to a titular Head of State surrounded by a structured system of committees and ministries, it followed that finance too was to evolve in application of these same structures of system inter-link, indeed, of that same philosophy that removed an individual man from the responsibility of power. What the politicians first failed to see, and then acquiesced in bringing about, was that finance was to take on a quite new identity, a new evolutionary growth, inspired certainly by greed but in fact a result of the complexification, extension and finally open-ended possibility of a wealth that had passed from the gold specie of the kings, to the Assignats in paper of the people, to the heady billions of a numbers wealth, circling the globe in seconds, and acquiring lands and nations as it flew round the world. In the popular media this new caste of financiers openly called themselves The Masters of the Universe.

What has to be understood is that this was nowhere grasped by the men who defined the political discourse. Not only nineteenth century thinkers failed to see the growing and enmeshing powers of finance, but it eluded the thinkers of the twentieth century. Certainly the failure of the Soviet State was the direct result of applied Marxist-Leninism's dialectical incapacity to understand banking capitalism and the relationship of political structure to personal authority. Yet these two issues remain today in the monosystem of democracy still unconfronted.

"The State must not interfere with the Market." This hidden codicil emerged more and more at the turn of the century. Still no-one dared point out that it meant that power had passed from the State to the Market. Therefore, whoever ruled the Market ruled the People. The State, the 'National' State was now national only in its government and its football team. Its finance had slipped the century's long moorings of nationalism and become enmeshed in the webbed structuring of banking and commodities acquisition. The more complex the legal framework of State and inter-State imperatives, the more elusive and hidden become the movement of wealth and therefore power. Balzac's 'Secret History' was not a matter of the modern fantasy called 'Conspiracy Theory' but rather its opposite, a set of new structures and methods and personnel about whom we, the People, were simply not being allowed to know.

Those who follow the leader become entirely lost. Once they grasp that great complex industrial countries clearly cannot be being ruled by a failed Hollywood actor or by a third-rate impeachable lawyer, as in America, or by an uninformed housewife or a mentally unstable lawyer, as in England, they begin to look for the key in the web of organisations – in other words, the Hidden Hand. He must be lurking in these ad hoc power groups of supra-national gatherings in remote hotels. Thus they end up, as it is hoped if not intended, in the maze of Conspiracy Theory.

Those who follow the poverty trail or the pollution trail become lost in ecological rescue attempts. There is so much to save, the rain forest, the polar ice-caps, the Lacandón Indians, and of course, the whale. Those who follow the money trail have even less chance, for here, the financiers have designed their own protection system in case of siege. The financial systems themselves are tied into a complex multi-layered system that only at key points solidifies into what we traditionally called 'capital'. The form of wealth is not anymore capitalist – it is a flow-wealth system that moves across frontiers, across corporation structures which melt into holding companies and wholly-owned subsidiaries. It disappears at point A, an inaccessible bank in the Bahamas, to re-surface as fissionable material in the desert, only to be lost in the activation of a design programme for a swing-wing supersonic fighter for a nation under sanctions. The listed ten richest men in the world are simply attendant players, far from being Prince Hamlet in this play of wealth.

The matter of this study is power. To this end what happened to it and how it metamorphosed at the time of the Great Dysjunction is its concern, and finally, its future shape. As at the beginning of the affair, 1789, so today, that concerns not only the domain of the man but the domain of the woman. For the accomplishment of the Great Dysjunction and its logical conclusion which transforms yesterday's free citizens into today's debtor consumers, two heads had to fall into the basket of the guillotine in the Place de la Revolution, sorry, Place de la Concorde.

Early in his masterwork, 'Du Pouvoir', Bertrand de Jouvenel unfolds the evolutionary character of State power.

"From the partitioning of the continent into kingdoms, the history of the West shows us an almost uninterrupted process of State growth. One can only be blind to it if one becomes concerned only with the forms of Power: a monarch is fantastically presented as master of all he demands without limit, then a representative regime is seen where the means available to the ruler are measured; and finally came democracy in which the general consentment only grants what it wants to a Power obedient to it.

"None of that is measurable. But what is, are the dimensions of the army, the amount of taxes, the number of civil servants. The physical importance of these instruments provides an exact indication of the growth of power. Begin with the State under Philippe Auguste (early 13th century). Absolutely no taxes maintain it, but like any other landowner the king lives off his domains. Absolutely no army under his command, but only some guards who eat from his table. No bureaucracy except the priests he employs and the servants to whom he assigns public duties. Even his Treasury, itself his own wealth, is left at the Temple in the hands of his banker monks. As his subject I would never meet the supreme lord, he would ask me no contribution, claim no military service from me, nor pass any law which could affect my existence.

"At the end of the reign of Louis XIV – what a change! By relentless secular means the People have been induced to fill the royal coffers on a regular basis. The monarch at his own expense runs a permanent army of two hundred thousand men. His Intendants force all the provinces into obedience; his police deal with the dissatisfied. He makes the laws, he persecutes those who do not pray the way he wants. A vast body of bureaucrats weaken and silence the nation. The will of the Power is imposed. The Power is no longer a point in the society but a stain at the centre, a network which resonates through its entirety.

"Is this excessive? Will the Revolution which overthrows the King demolish his edifice, attack the apparatus of command, at least destroy it in part – to reduce the tribute paid by the People?

"Certainly not! It will introduce the conscription desired by the monarchy but which it did not have the force to impose. It is true that one will no more see the (Royalist) budgets of Calonne: for they will be doubled under Napoleon and tripled under the Restoration. The Intendant will have disappeared, but will have been replaced by the Prefect. And the expansion will continue. From régime to régime, more soldiers, more taxes, more laws, more bureaucrats."

The astonishingly modern Tocqueville, blandly assumed to be the great apologist for democracy, was far from taken in, for example in his 'On Democracy in America' he stated:

"They recovered centralisation from its ruins and restored it, and at the same time that they raised it up again, all that had formerly limited it remained destroyed, and from the very entrails of a nation that had just overthrown royalty one was to see suddenly emerge a more extended power, more detailed, more absolute than that which had been exercised by any of our kings."

In 'L'Ancien Régime' he stated, noting the collapse of the aristocratic ethos as an end to the ethical 'noblesse oblige':

"In the ancient feudal society, if the lord possessed great rights, he also had great responsibilities. It was for him to rescue the indigents in the interior of his domains. We find a last trace of the old legislation of Europe in the Prussian Code of 1795 where it states: 'The Lord must see to it that the poor peasants receive an education. They must, as much as possible, procure living means for those of their vassals who own no land. If some among them fall into indigence, he is obliged to come to their rescue.'"

Jouvenel is scathing about the philosophers who hold up to men their perfect societies, their republics, their utopias where disorder and injustice are banished. From Plato to Thomas More they outline the utopian fantasy.

"Common the land: the magistrates will divide up for the citizens what they need. Uniform the clothing, a common meal, a common dwelling-house. The tasks to be assigned by the magistrates, and to apply for studies, the always reversible consent of the same magistrates.

"More divided the existence of his Utopians between agricultural work and an urban profession, to be decided by the father unless decided otherwise by the magistrates. None could leave home without a passport confirming the date of return. ... If you look for liberty you will not find it. All these dreams are of tyrannies, narrower, heavier, and more oppressive than any which history has yet shown."

From Savonarola to Calvin, he comments, the philosophers search for the man of action, the temporal arm of power as Plato waited for the tyrant of Syracuse to put into force his laws.

Voltaire, he notes, found it wonderful that Catherine the Great, in his words, "...could force fifty-thousand men to march on Poland to establish tolerance and liberty of conscience."

So, today, the tyrants march forth, supported in their projects of extended Power, supported by a whole media-backed philosophical grooming, to devastate two ancient cultures, Iraq and Afghanistan, for the high task of – precisely the same ends – tolerance and liberty of conscience, only now the fifty-thousand have become hundreds of thousands backed up by massive air power to reduce the population to submission, 'Shock and Awe', assuring rescue. Jouvenel writes:

"Such is the natural evolution of a people who set out to police others. ... At the decisive battle of the 14th century, Poitiers, around fifty thousand men faced each other. About as many at Marignano. Scarcely more, sixty-five thousand they say at Nordlingen, the decisive battle of the Thirty Years War. But already two hundred thousand at Malplaquet (1709) and four hundred and fifty thousand at Leipzig (1813).

"Now we do better. The 1914 war mutilated or killed five times as many men as all of Europe had under arms at the end of the Napoleonic Wars. ...

We have finished up where the savages began, we have re-discovered the lost art of starving non-combatants, of burning their homes and of leading them, defeated, into slavery. What need do we have of barbaric invasions? We are our own Huns."

Bertrand de Jouvenel had no doubt about the turning point, that point which broke with set-piece battlefield wars of armies to create super-armies that could sweep across countries, in other words a new system leading to total war.

On 23 August 1793 it took the Convention to issue a Proclamation which no former monarch would have dared to impose.

"From this moment up until that time when all our enemies have been driven from the territory of the Republic, all Frenchmen are permanently requisitioned for army service."

In 1794 one million one hundred and sixty nine thousand men were under French military control.

Jouvenel: "A new era had opened in military history, that of cannon fodder. No general of the Ancien Régime would have dared to throw his men in deep columns under enemy fire. When Folard had proposed it no-one would let him be heard. ... The generals of the Revolution and the Empire spent without counting. Power drew out from the whole French Nation what they asked for, and history can say that from these massacres began the decline of the population and the energy of France.

"In 1798 the Jourdan Law formed this human requisition into a system. Men from twenty to twenty-five, five classes showing a million men, were obliged to serve, the law was to decide how many of them were to be called up and the selection would indicate the conscripts. Each year an older class could be recalled and a younger one called up. It was the system Napoleon was to use: first one sees him take eighty thousand men in each class, up until, in preparation for the Russian campaign, he called one hundred and twenty thousand men from the class of 1810, until after the disasters one sees him call up one hundred and fifty thousand men of the class of 1814 and recuperate three hundred thousand men from the classes which before he had used sparingly. In total, from September 1805 up to November 1813, he had asked of France two million one hundred thousand men more than the soldiers the Republic kept on duty.

"How could Europe fight if it did not have recourse to similar practices?"

Jouvenel's relentless examination continues:

"However, Germany learned nothing from this experience. Alone among the victorious powers which had forced France to abandon that system by which it had laid waste to Europe, Prussia kept for herself a similar system, even worse, which prepared for the victories of 1870. This success appalled Europe, forcing all the continental countries to follow Germany's example of adopting conscription. With this excellent result by 1888 the armies on a peace footing had the same total as at the height of the Napoleonic Wars, three million men. The public spending of the European States which amounted to 170 million pounds sterling in 1816 had passed 868 million by 1898.

"Finally the storm broke: one knows the result. Eight million dead, six million disabled. Among the belligerent European countries, 8% of the male productive force destroyed, in France and Germany 10%."

Jouvenel's phrase, "The demonstration was then made a second time", indicates the validity of his thesis which is that a society founded on the myths of the People's representation by elected parliamentarians, senators and congressmen, in effect assures that Power, not being under their command, finds its executors and drives relentlessly on, conflict after conflict, towards an inescapable catastrophe, unless – unless the logical sequence is broken by a new community of excellence operating under a quite new set of values.

Jouvenel makes it clear:

"Thus, since the Middle Ages, to uphold the political struggles, the States increased the sacrifices that they demanded of their nations. So while the Capetians (France's Royal House) made war with lordly contingents which they could utilise only for forty days, the People's States of today have the mastery to call up and keep indefinitely under arms the whole male population. While the feudal monarchs had to sustain their conflicts uniquely with the resources of their domains, their inheritors can dispose of the whole national revenue. It was possible for the people of the medieval cities to ignore the war as long as they were at a distance from the theatre of operations. Today enemies and allies burn their houses, massacre their families and measure their exploits by ravaged hectares. Thinking itself, formerly disdainful of these conflicts, is now mobilised in the service of these operations of conquest, obliged to proclaim the civilising virtue of the gunners and the incendiaries.

"How is it possible to fail to recognise in this prodigious degradation of our civilisation, the fruits of the absolutist State? Everything is thrown into the war because now Power can utilise everything."

Jouvenel indicates that the people have no defender. Those who are the State reserve for them alone the right to speak in the name of the Nation, not admitting any interest of the Nation other than the interest of the State. They crush as sedition what the monarchy welcomed as remonstrance. Under the pretext that the Power had been given to the Nation, and because it refuses to recognise that there are there two distinct entities which can never cease to be thus, the Nation has been given up to the Power.

The French Revolution, child of these philo-sophers seen as so dangerous by Jouvenel – Voltaire and Rousseau – was also led by two political leaders directly inspired both by the Platonic Republic in its theoretical purity and by

Sparta with its cult of male militarism voided of female compassion. The specific nature of what happened in France's Revolution has been established as the transfer of power from the monarch to 'the Nation', and this total deception with its high rhetoric of Power to the People and even the Will of the People has seen the elevation of a structuralist system of State which then presents itself as synonymous and co-terminous with the Nation. The term 'Republic', in other words, is chosen to represent the claimed unity of State and Nation.

Jouvenel adds a further dimension to his perception of the post-Revolutionary State that followed the abolition of monarchy as culminating in an absolutist State by taking into account something he finds common to every Revolution.

"Violent crises in the movement of institutions, political revolutions hold the attention of the historians. The sudden flame of smouldering passions, the explosion and the fiery propagation of principles which had spread underground, the deployment of individuals in brutal and unpremeditated actions, the monstrous tumult of the mob which swiftly obliterates the grave faces of professional men to raise them up as terrifying masks of animal cruelty, what exalted material for the writer and what an occasion for thrills it offers to the reader comfortable at his fireside.

"These periods are the most retold, but also the least understood. The intelligence of man remains childish and the learning quite often entertains rather than teaches. Sensitive to the appearance of events, they are being understood by recognising the wave as being the movement of the sea, while the current has not been measured. People cling to the cry of 'Liberty!' which resounds at the beginning of every revolution, and fail to notice that there is none that does not fall before the crushing weight of Power. In order to grasp the true role of revolutions, to assign to these rapids and sudden falls a true place in the immense flow of History, one must avoid being fascinated by their turbulence, but look away, observe what the speed of the river was before it took on this hurtling movement, and how it behaves after these events are over.

"Before, it was the authority of Charles I, of Louis XVI, and Nicholas II. After, it was the authority of Cromwell, of Napoleon, and Stalin. These are the masters which the People submitted to, the masters they raised up against the 'tyranny' of Stuart, of Bourbon and of Romanoff.

"The phenomenon is dazzling: it is a false

interpretation! Alas, they say, the Revolution was distracted, the anti-social overflowing of liberty called up a restraining force which obliged a discipline, the reactionaries were to blame for so much ruin that a reconstructor was necessary! Ah! If only such an error had been avoided, or such another! So much ingenuity is spent to discover the exact moment of licentiousness, to specify the notorious act, to name the one responsible.

"Pitiful incomprehension! Profound misunderstanding of the nature of the revolutionary phenomenon! No, the Cromwells and the Stalins are not fortuitous consequences, unexpected accidents during the social tempest, but rather the fatal end to which the overthrow was leading in a necessary way: the cycle opens with the shattering of a weak Power but does not close until it is replaced by the most absolute Power."

He backs up his case with detailed analyses of the Stuarts and how the light 'shipmoney tax' which sparked the Revolution was soon replaced by Cromwell with taxes ten times greater. The King had endured Parliament, Cromwell dismissed it. Only now in the twenty-first century can Nicholas II and Louis XVI be examined with anything like a fair assessment. What do we find?

In 'Nicholas II' by Hélène d'Encausse the case is plainly put.

"For the Bolsheviks, Nicholas II was 'The Bloodthirsty'. For his family, for his contemporaries, for a number of historians, he was 'a weak man, without a project,' and Freud saw him as neurotic."

Encausse questions this and recognises something else as well. In his time she perceived a slow and reluctant but decisive movement towards liberalisation and reform. The assassination of Stolypin politically took away that last chance of a monarchic transformation, just as Mirabeau's death broke the last link between monarch and social change.

In 'Louis XVI', Jean-Christian Petitfils takes a new measure of Louis. The biographer notes the similarities between Louis and Nicholas, and accepts the comparison of Mme. Encausse. Again the reformist moves by the monarch, the abolition of torture, the moves to open the economy by Turgot, then Necker, then Calonne. The resistance of the King to the Nobility, then the failure of all by his reluctance to enforce his will, to command. Both Encausse and Petitfils confirm the political insight of Jouvenel:

"Thus the renovation and the re-enforcement of Power appears as the true historical function of revolutions. Finish then with those salutations to the spirit of liberty rising against an oppressor Power. They are so few and one cannot cite one that overthrew a real despot.

"Did the People rise up against Louis XIV? No, but against the nice old Louis XVI, who would not let his own Swiss bodyguards fire. Against Peter the Great? No, but against the simple-minded Nicholas II who could not even be avenged for losing his dear Rasputin. ... They died, these Kings, not because of their tyranny but because of their weakness. The People prepare the scaffold not as a moral punishment for despotism but as a biological sanction against powerlessness."

What has been established in the course of this study is that the transfer of power that took place with the Great Dysjunction was not the passing from one man to another. The changes effected resulted in a new kind of society, the obliteration of the old, and an abstract political discourse to replace a behavioural pattern in which the Noblesse held an ethical obligation to the poor and the poor could, by it, maintain a respect for an aristocratic class. With the same force that monarchy was brutally ended, the masses too,

Noblesse and Plebeians were levelled. All were citizens now. In order for the return to zero, everything that had belonged to the centuries of personal rule, of feudal obligation and restraint, of provincial governance, with the sustaining and disciplining forces of gentry and clergy, all, all had to be swept away. Everything and everybody stood facing unique and unbridled power. It was the great liquidation of counter-powers. Mirabeau, the realist, observed: "The idea of forming only one class of citizens would have pleased Richelieu, this level surface makes easy the exercise of power."

From then on, in France, and quickly all over the world came the application of the method that was the Aristotelian Politique. With abolition of the monarchy, both the man and the woman, thereafter, the odd couple Robespierre and Saint-Just, could enforce their classical and pure, i.e. logical system. Religion without compassion – a Supreme Being, itself a grid of measured obligations. A new decimal calendar, a geometrising of France itself – a Hexagon! Sieyès wanted the country cut into eighty rectangular zones.

Benjamin Constant warned: "The systematic mind is immediately drawn to symmetry. The love of Power soon discovered what an enormous advantage this symmetry could provide." Everything that had been called 'The Enlightenment' became the in-back theoretical frame for the new society. A crude scientism gave legitimacy to the new legislated totalitarianism. It was not a passing enthusiasm or a superficial rhetoric to be replaced by genuine existential discourse. Washington, the new American capital was laid out on the strictest geometric, indeed masonic principles. New York was a chess-board of numbered streets, dissected by equally numbered avenues.

In the 21st century Frédéric Cathala wrote a novel, 'Les Mille Mots du Citoyen Morille Marmouset' in which a Republican enflamed by the Revolutionary ethos invents a thousand-word 'Onomasticon' – a lexicon for the new society. He explains, boasting it will have not one synonym: "...united in the same comprehension of a unique discourse. Firstly, the neo-French will triumph over the weak, degenerate and decadent dialects. They are obstacles to clear thinking. Language of enlightenment, neo-French will soon supplant all the languages in the world. A unique language for perfect harmony across the whole surface of the Earth!"

Of course, the precision of the satire lies in the

two twentieth century inventions, having the same aim: Basic English, an exact replica, and Esperanto, a totally invented 'world' language.

Also at the heart of the rationalist cult is the necessary 'abolition' of women. The tactic, the successful tactic of reason was to turn them into citizens, and as such into pseudo-men, or, more precisely, women who would submit to being inside the political system grid. Mention has already been made of the Convention's unanimous vote (9 Brumaire, Year 2) decreeing the abolition of the women's political club. Later, subsumed under 'humans', they would be allowed into the political discourse. In Cathala's satire he relates:

"'Two miserable women, one Olympe de Gouges and one Theroigne de Mericourt have made a demand. The first had even drawn up a Declaration of the Rights of Women... A Declaration of the Rights of Women, can you imagine...!'
'And what did they do to these furies?'
'The first has been condemned and executed for her madness. The second has been nearly whipped to death by a justly outraged crowd. She is now locked up in Charenton...'"

Here, of course, he was relating history, his theme being that the Revolution in many aspects is itself surreal. His footnote informs us that Mericourt died in 1817 without ever having been liberated!

The whole doctrinal programme of wiping out the past and starting a new society which is the ethos of the Revolution allows Cathala to create a genuine satire in the best Swiftian tradition by founding his fiction on the historical follies of Revolutionary fervour, something that was to recreate itself in 1917 Russia. His mockery of the decision to revise the deck of playing cards to reflect the abolition of king and court needs no invention, reality had become its own satire. The King had been replaced by the Philosopher. It was decreed by the Convention, 12 October 1792.

He deftly dismantles the foundational doctrines and vocabulary of Rousseau on which the whole edifice of the new democratic society was to be founded.

"'The savages who ate Captain Cook, were they good?' asked the young boy. 'Without a doubt, for man in the state of nature is naturally good,' replied the little girl in her most serious tone.

'And Captain Cook, was he good?'

'Of course Captain Cook was good, otherwise the savages would not so quickly have eaten him all up!'"

As Cathala's comic characters are precipitated to their tragic end on the scaffold the vital issues are tremblingly recognised, if too late:

"'Man? Your Revolution speaks a lot about Man. But I only know some men and perhaps, with the help of experience, I will end up knowing 'men'. But Man? Forcibly to introduce the Universal into the particular, the abstract into the concrete, it is to force the square into the circle: you must either saw up one or quarter the other. Your Revolution is the bed of Procrustes: an instrument of torture and death.'"

Let it be recalled to a generation robbed of a classical education by the new education which depends on cutting off all knowledge of the past:

"Procrustean: of or pertaining to Procrustes, aiming or tending to produce uniformity by violent or arbitrary methods.

Procrustes: a fabulous robber of Attica who made his victims conform to the length of his bed by stretching or mutilation."

(Shorter Oxford Dictionary, II, 1678)

So it was that the post-Revolutionary State emerged as absolute. Stripped of all the interlocking balances and inhibitions of the old system, and with its élite class eliminated, the aristocracy, it soon required for its legalist basis a new governing class, the statocracy. Yet the new bureaucratic class was assured its performance by virtue of its stasis, its pyramidic solidity. It could not threaten the State as the aristocracy once threatened and inhibited monarchy. It was another element of the social nexus which had broken free that was soon, by a rapid evolutionary process, to take over the newly established leadership of law. The Sect, as Proudhon defined them, the bankers, emerged swiftly and vividly as an increasingly dominant group. With the abolition of the aristocracy the First Estate, the Nobility, were transformed into the statocracy, led by the self-rewarding system of the Universal Franchise. Representational power once engineered was absolute power. At the same time, however, the Clergy, or Second Estate, were abolished. The State was defined as secular. This never for a moment meant that it was deemed necessary to abolish the strange doctrines of Divine anthropophagy – reason and the philosophers could handle this. No. The 'Clergy', in France, meant Richelieu and Mazarin, it was the primal banking system which had emerged as Power more and more needed to 'purchase'. The 'secular' State found that its new élite of bankers, which were to emerge over the next two centuries, took as its credo: "The State must not interfere with the Market." The Power had passed from the lawyers and their bureaucracy to the bankers and their initiate personnel. The 'Market' was the coded name for the amalgamated system that had transformed the term 'purchase' into a volatile system of webbed commerce. Once 'currency' was seen as a tradable commodity it was able to absorb into its movement all the commodities that men wanted to buy and sell. As the currency system englobed the exchange of goods, trade in effect transformed into distribution.

It suited the Sect that the reformist discourse, following Marxist methodology, identified the 'enemy' as being the multi-national corporations, this both kept the dialectic healthily anti-capitalist but at the same time indicated a global enemy that had no identity, no form and no face. The Marxist in the end was a mere Luddite, did anyone really want to abolish computers or the pharmaceutical industry? The secretive nature of the Sect was an essential part not only of its power but of its fear. Only now are the veils being lifted – the Salomé of banking is dancing for the head of Jokaanan, the political leader.

II

So it was that two hundred years after the rupture
with human society as it had always been constituted, that is, personal rule under Divine governance, the atheist-humanist system now under a
new generic title, democracy, began its inevitable
and shameful collapse.

Chateaubriand defined it clearly: "L'aristocratie
a trois âges successifs: l'âge de supériorités, l'âge
des privilèges, l'âge des vanités: sortie du premier,
elle dégénère dans le second, et s'éteint dans le
dernier."

He saw that form, while stretching into the distant past, as a cruel reality of which he was the witness. In its immediate reality, Louis XIII saw the imposition of a long forged aristocracy, Louis XIV saw both the forging of a formal élite and its rewards, along with the degeneration so crisply delineated by Saint Simon. Louis XV at the end of his reign opened the final phase. Significantly, his first consort was a Queen, his second a cultured and gifted courtesan, and his third taken from the streets of Paris where she would leave her guillotined head in the misogynist fury of the Revolution he foretold – "Après moi – le déluge!"

In England – there had never been a Britain – the aristocracy, which had cast out its legitimate ruling monarchy, to control the island itself with only a puppet monarch destined uniquely to the laying of wreaths, the cutting of ceremonial ribbons, and the smashing of champagne bottles against the hulls of ships, was to last longer. Its first phase was what has been openly called the Whig Supremacy, that is the successful aristocratic rule under the Hanovers. Its second phase was that of the reign of the bastard Queen Victoria, sired by a courtier. The Boer War heralded its final phase, bringing the last riches of the Victorian Age in gold and diamonds, and heralding the fatal allegiance of politics to banking, setting Oppenheimer, Bait, de Beers and Barnato alongside Milner, and Edward, Lord Cecil of that great family which established itself under Elizabeth I and was to supervise the dismantling of the hereditary House of Lords under a Prime Minister, lackey of global finance, under Elizabeth II.

Its final phase came in World War I which saw the sons of the ruling class decimated on Flanders fields, then the hysteria of the 1920s was to give way to the final collapse. The last ruling aristocrat (that is, taking the parliament with him in consensus) was Winston Churchill who turned all the ignominies of World War II into poetic triumphs. The retreat from Dunkirk and the sacrifice by his choice of the Highland Division saw the withdrawal from Continental Europe, and the return invasion under the American flag. A second invasion of Europe by America was to indicate the shape of things to come. The imperial project became an enacting of a (divinely!) Manifest Destiny liberating lands from monarchy, dictatorship and primitivism. The genocidal murderers of the great Navaho and Mohawk nations were ready to repeat their triumphal technological victories worldwide. However, the machinery, the political machinery that drove, that is, both drove and fuelled, the 'democratic' project was no longer the class of lawyers and politicians prior to 1945. It was the new élite. It was that Sect about which the retiring war hero and general, President Eisenhower, had warned an unheeding nation: the Military-Industrial Complex. Still, then, no-one had grasped that this new Sect was headed by the financial élite, except for one American poet whose similar warning had him locked and imprisoned in a monkey-cage and declared insane lest he testify his evidence – Ezra Pound.

The Sect, to maintain Proudhon's term, which had been both evolving and gaining ascendancy over the ruling political élite, were to emerge after 1945 as the undisputed, because unidentified, ruling élite on an almost world level of control, philosophy and system.

The nature of the Sect's power is based uniquely on the complex and interlocking elements enmeshing abstract numbers currency, commodities, and computerised transfer systems. Its superiority is in no way based on a morally or intellectually or physically superior group – for although they today represent all that is most despicable and valueless in men, this in no way reflects their own predecessors in the Sect. The founders of the Sect, the creators of the great European and American financial system and banks were a cultured and honourable body of men, albeit a closed society self-designed to be a carbon copy of a league of christian patriots. They left behind not only family fortunes brilliantly structured to avoid the death duties inflicted on their host nation's élite, but also whole museums of collected art offered up to the nation which they had done so well by, and who did not even know by what financial methods they had acquired the paintings, sculptures and furniture of their own, that is the nation's forebears.

Before examining the phenomenology of the financial world it is necessary to outline the salient points of banking's transformative growth.

1. An ex-nihilo system of currency, first in paper specie, later simply as a numbers system transferred electronically. As banker Dr Shalabi of Iraq defined it, "Now money is an electronic impulse passing between computer terminals."
2. Banking Houses run by particular families on a hereditary basis.
3. Networking of inter-bank wealth by marriages, family appointments and

assimilation of most gifted usurers.

4. The Breton Woods Agreement establishing the hegemony of the U.S. dollar.

5. The link between gold and dollar price broken by President Nixon.

6. The introduction of 24 hour trading made permissible by computer technology.

7. The end of the capital-based bank serving State and personal clients: a system dependent on advisory fiduciary practice.

8. The emergence of the brokerage house as bank and corporation.

9. The control of all commodities by manipulating corporate structures measured as instruments of financial value or potential growth. Leveraged buy-outs.

10. A banking system in near-global control through mergers and acquisitions.

11. Trade transformed into mobile profit mechanisms based on ecological indifference and military dominance of opposition.

12. Cities, ports and countries are now acquired as commodities once were.

13. The movement of trade is now co-terminous with the movement of money.

14. A futures market with unrealisable formulae moves inexorably to collapse.

15. It is illegal to export gold from the USA.

It is this rapid evolutionary impulse since the opportunity of 1945 that simply is not allowed into the public discourse. The reality that power has passed from the political class to the Sect, who had become responsible for the formative development of the social order, had to be kept from both the masses and the tiny educated élite. So successfully hidden was it that the situation demanded an explanation for the public perception that in fact a massive shift in wealth and ownership was in process.

The tactical solutions of the swiftly emerging new power group were twofold. The first was the confrontation of the recognition that 'something was going on' in secret. Inquiring journalism could not forever be kept at bay. The Great Wall of protection soon was erected. The perception of financial interlink, transfer of wealth, staged invasions was designed for public consumption as 'a conspiracy'. Hidden collaborations, appropriations and politico-economic common interest were then publicly displayed as 'Conspiracy Theory'.

Orson Welles once gave the present author the definition of both neurosis and psychosis. He said that if it seemed that every time you arrived in a foreign city hotel there were men drilling noisily outside your window – that was neurosis. Once you looked out your window and claimed it was the same men in every city – that was psychosis.

With a new plethora of supra-national institutions and private groupings hosted in private venues by important public figures, with Bilderbergers, Club de Rome, Club de Paris, Club Galilée, Pérouse Commission, it was easy to turn the turbulent and indeed emerging forms of finance into a singular phenomenon, a spider's web, and that implied a spider. Easily people saw it all as a great conspiracy and that meant that at its heart was a hidden power élite, a concealed leader and a hidden agenda of global domination. One could say that Conspiracy Theory was the fantastical movie version of a real event utterly misunderstood. It was not like they said, but once they said it – clearly, it was paranoia. Let ordinary sane people forget the whole affair, that was the message.

The second tactic of distraction from the quite astonishing effulgence of banking-finance and banking itself becoming both the fuel and the machine of world trade, was specific, individual, and directed at the psychological identity of the urban individual. Rome, to divert the Plebeians from the burgeoning wealth of the élite, gave the masses bread and circuses. The modern version was as follows: to distract people from desiring economic freedom, the right to choose your medium of exchange, freedom from purchase tax, interest, credit profile – something intrinsically human had to fill the void created by financial slavery. In place of it was offered sexual liberty. Bonded and enslaved by debt, mortgaged, and crippled by interest rates, the individual was offered sexual liberation. Basically the human creature was free to 'explore his or her sexuality'. Anything was permitted. Unfortunately for the world, the removal of all sexual taboos opened up an anomalous forbidden zone, the molestation of children. Unfortunately, for given the nature of man, and thus the lie of humanism, once something is forbidden, it becomes desirable.

Sexuality became a private estate which the individual could govern at will. His own estate, land itself, had been acquired by a corporation to grow genetically modified crops, his house on the estate was mortgaged to the hilt, his business was bankrupt, inflation devalued daily the money left in his pocket. Yet each day movies, celebrities and media assured him – his sexuality was his own. The word never existed among the Greeks, it was a purely 20th century coinage, like the epoch's coinage itself, utterly worthless.

What then was the action of the power élite that obliged it to adopt such a disturbing, protective set of tactics, of such far-reaching consequences that it could be said they changed the fundamental anthropology of the human species, alienating them perhaps irretrievably from nature?

It is not necessary to make even a primitive analysis of banking capitalism to recognise the true identity of the bankers. The famous slogan of the Gun Lobby in the USA, "Guns do not kill people – people do," must be applied in the same way here. "Banks do not endebt and cheat people – bankers do."

As the veil has here been drawn back to gaze at the executioners and victims of the Great Dysjunction caused by the Terror, now it must be pulled back to expose the phenomenology of the Sect.

André Meyer, who reconstructed the Lazard Investment Bank after 1945, announced the rule of their House. "The secret of the House, is the secret." While members of the Stock Exchange and business are regularly exposed to the media, and the Rothschilds because of their long historical leadership, often exaggerated, are open to some scrutiny, the former head of Lazard and his important associates, who count among the most influential men on the planet, remain completely unknown. So it was that in the traditional Banking Houses that emerged in the ruins of Europe, the Sect could at last create first its presence, then its influence, and finally its dominance over the political class.

The place of that institution of private wealth, the Investment Bank, lay between economics and politics. Bernard Esambert, former Rothschild banker, stated: "It is at the junction of the State apparatus and the private sector that the possibilities of making money are the greatest."

The investment banks, the private and discreet institutions of private and State wealth, had evolved an internal system of both behaviour and social connection. There was a code of conduct, social conduct, in business affairs, and a web of connectedness, not merely an inter-bank linkage but the protective ties of marriage and family.

Secrecy was the motto not just of Lazard but of

all the great Banking Houses, no wonder the anxious debtors saw it as one huge conspiratorial secret. Speaking of the French banker, Alain Wertheimer, a close confidant said, "The guy is secretive by nature. He is sincerely secretive. It is a line of conduct for him, to such a point that it is nearly a philosophy." Of the Spanish banking family March it was said they practised what Buñuel had ironically named 'the discreet charm of the bourgeoisie'. They keep away from fashionable events, they stay out of the glossy magazines. The tribe stay sealed off, unfathomable and without any rough edges, like their headquarters, a cube of white marble with rounded edges. Alfonso Piñiero, their biographer, relates:

"Around them no-one speaks. They are surrounded by a wall of sepulchral silence. ... They have adopted the discretion and the prudence of their grandfather. With these methods but under different circumstances they have followed the same line: gain money by adapting to the ethical norms of the time."

By these means, which were only made possible by a dynastic system, the March family have not merely survived but amassed billions over the last century, flourishing through two kings, a republic, two dictators, several coups, a civil war, a transition and then political democracy. In Spain they are seen as more than the Nation State, they call them the Planet March.

The public record of the March Foundation exposes to view a further tactic of the Sect to distract, deliberately distract from their true occupation, profession and passion, the acquiring and increase of their own wealth. The two preferred roles of the Sect are as patrons and philanthropists.

March Foundation mounted the first Picasso Exhibition in Spain since the Civil War – an exhibition hosted by Franco's banker! In July 1936 Juan March financed the landing of Franco in Spain aboard a small De Havilland Dragon Rapide aeroplane. March left for Portugal in 1941 but returned to join the great Franquist families, to serve the dictatorship. He moved smoothly from Fascist State to Transition to Democracy. If his work, his professional banking, was done in the salons of the Pardo he offered to the Spanish people the generous art patron mounting exhibitions and acquiring contemporary paintings.

Jacques Wertheimer acquired, with superb taste and counsel, the collages of Max Ernst, the paintings of Douanier Rousseau, Dégas, Nicolas de Staël, masks from Benin, antiques from Egypt. Two floors of a skyscraper in Manhattan at 9 West 57th Street were rented as the base of his U.S. activities, and to house his Collection.

His father before him had started collecting works of art. Pierre Wertheimer, painted by Boldini, bought out of his enormous wealth Monet, Picasso, Matisse, Pissarro, Vlaminck, and from his preferred artist, Soutine, he purchased 16 paintings.

Lazard's David-Weill was a compulsive collector. "A day never passed but he bought a work of art," was the observation of his son, Michel David-Weill. Fragonard, Watteau, Goya, Chardin, Corot, Delacroix, Ingrès, Dégas – David-Weill instructed, "This painting for me, that one for the museum." He 'gifted' to the museums of L'Orangerie, Carnavalet and the Louvre. In this way he was appointed to the governing bodies of national museums and was named as a member of the Academy of Beaux-Arts. Marcel Proust had attended the Condorcet Lycée with David-Weill. Proust, a close friend of Horace Finaly, Director of the Bank of Paris, remembered his banker school-mate and so sent him a copy of 'À l'ombre des jeunes filles en fleurs' at the same time as he sent copes to Edmond and Robert de Rothschild. When Pierre David-Weill, the son of David David-Weill, took over the Lazard enterprise his other son, Jean, became a curator of the Louvre, responsible for Islamic Arts, a department to which his family had made important donations.

This role of art collector and patron became the underside of the public face that the bankers offered to the masses to gain not merely their admiration but their gratitude. They wanted to be seen as generous. Their profession was taking. Their persona was giving. They, with an admirable lack of shame, declared they were philanthropists. By the end of the twentieth century the term 'philanthropist' had simply become a synonym for 'banker'.

The visit by a member of the senior aristocratic family of Beaumont to the Camondo bankers' museum in the old bankers' district of the Parc Monceau, which houses the acquired in a lifetime collection of mostly 18th century furniture and artefacts, filled her with dismay. As she strolled among the Louis XVI and Louis XV she suddenly saw the true irony of the generous gift, the Camondo Museum, to the 'People' of Paris: "But these things belonged to everyone we know." When they had been the power élite these were the bi-products of their rule, signs of a high civilisation. "Chairs we sat in, dishes we ate from..." now safely behind a silken cord lest the debtor-public which had paid its entrance fee should sit upon these chairs. Giving back as generosity what had been acquired by deception, returning a portion of their ill-gained wealth to the bankrupted generations forced to yield an ancient inheritance to the usurious collectors.

The modalities of banking change while the foundational elements do not. The underlying instrument of the financial system remains that of the French Revolution's Assignat. The instrument or token of wealth, in other words, is not wealth itself but rather a receipt or a token which validates a purchase or exchange. This has metamorphosed itself from simple promissory note to letter of credit, to cheque-book, to credit card, to coded numbers transmitted and stored in computer systems. To clarify the extent of this transformation it is enough to say that there would be small pickings if you were to raid a bank, what you would be required to do is hack into a computer pro- gramme, the task of the contemporary thief.

It becomes clear when one finally breaks down this underlying element of the financial system, the move from real-wealth currency, gold and silver, or any valued and accepted means of exchange to one of mere tokens, finally reduced to a mathematical coding, that what is being actuated is fraud. A deception. The pretence that the bankers are merely operating within a historical continuum that has always existed does not bear examination. On the contrary the historical record makes uneasy reading for the Sect, and invites cynicism as a response. The doctrine of usury, interest or increase on the loan, the motor oil of the receipt-in-motion, was declared illegal and forbidden in judaism, christianity and Islam. To license usury meant that atheism was an obligatory bi-product. It follows that the Sect are well aware of the illusory technique, the quasi-magical method of their art.

In Martine Orange's study of the Lazard Bank, 'Ces Messieurs de Lazard', she unmasks the continued role-playing of the Lazard family, bankers as gentry, bankers as art-collectors, bankers as discreet political advisors, bankers as guides to business projects, and in the end arrives at forcing from them how they view 'the transaction'. From Hubert Heilbronne, a Lazard associate of over forty years with the House, she elicits a smiling admission: "...without relying on the application of the famous principle: (André Meyer's famous rule: 'The secret of Lazard, that is the secret') since these mysteries are beyond us, we pretend to be their organisers."

And from Antoine Bernheim, Orange lays bare the astonishing admission: "Power is an abstract notion. It only exists in the measure that it is recognised by others."

And from Michel David-Weill she extracts the philosophical jewel: "Power is a reflection in a mirror. It is something that is loaned to you, but does not exist." Like the dollar in your pocket? Like the World Bank? Like the whole set of procedures in their new evolved system? Mergers? Acquisitions? Leveraged buy-outs? Futures markets?

The attitude of the Sect to religion is purely pragmatic. Whatever familial connection they may feel to a particular religion they are in equal measure inhibited by religion's doctrinal opposition or at least disapproval of the sophisticated web of a financial system based on hiding the usurious codicil. Atheism is the genuine position of the Sect – the Assignat was able to come into existence only because the State had abolished Catholicism and founded the pseudo-religion of

Robespierre and Rousseau's Supreme Being, a Divinity without moral laws. The Oppenheimers of South Africa embraced christianity. David David-Weill in 1945 converted to Catholicism. Jean-Marie Rouart of the Académie Française in 'Mes Fauves' enquired of Serge Dassault:

"Have you become Catholic like your father converted?" Dassault replied: "When you live in a country you must adopt the religion of the country. In a Muslim country one must be a Muslim. When one lives in a Catholic country like France, one must be a Catholic. That's my position."

Such a doctrine is abhorrent to the rabbi, the priest and the Imam. It is, of course, a key doctrine of freemasonry. Written in the Masonic Lodge of Washington on the wall is their declaration of faith: "We play at being believers." This is pure atheism. The Sect only has a token allegiance to religion as such. Hitler, Franco and Stalin have all played host to the now democratic/liberal Sect, currently wedded to the new creed of Tolérance.

If the character of the Sect members was able to continue its affair, the increase of wealth and the acquisitions that wealth allow, it must be recognised that they were able also to adapt to the changing modalities of financial method. Wars and disasters modulated the dominant key of a specific passage of time in their affairs, but so too did changing methods of money transfer, storage and record. If the masses scarcely noticed their own evolving relationship with banking, permitted bank account overdraft, cheque-book, credit card, and mortgage, they were even less aware of the meaning of computerised archive, 24-hour stock trading, currency trading and supra-national banks. So radical do the changes continue to be that it is tempting to say that the usurers of yesterday may be viewed as moral in relation to the high oligarchy of today. Nevertheless, it must be remembered that the great transition from the passive banking epoch to the frenzied market of today was initiated by one of the most respected and traditional of the historically established Houses. The only difference between the old investment banker and the modern merchant banker is style, a loss of style, accompanied by an enormous increase in profits.

Bruce Wasserstein, one of the new 'barbarians' long before he got his hands on Lazard, said: "Lazard were the first powerful House of Mergers and Acquisitions." In 1967 Lazard had embarked on actively involving itself in a profound reorganisation of capitalism through transforming both its projects and its personnel. They moved from the private client and his projects into the world of Mergers and Acquisitions. Euralux, La France Assurances, Viniprix, Euromarché, Generali, LVMH – and these were just the beginning. The Sect had entered the Market.

Lazard's first move was on December 21, 1968. They were to be the fiduciary backing for a tiny glass manufacturer, BSN, in its offer to purchase Saint-Gobain, a monument of industrial France, involved also in nuclear fuel and petroleum. A three hundred year old company that had served Louis XIV and Colbert.

The hostile OPA was like the introduction of the tank into trench warfare. And like the tank its first appearance failed. The OPA, the Ownership Participation Agreement, one form of leveraged buy-out, heralded a new age of commercial warfare. It required the Bank to step into the public arena in a way it had never, or at least rarely, done.

It was during this time that deliberate conditioning of the masses was seen as a necessary 'covering fire' for the tremendous spread of banking activity. The High Street Bank, as it was romantically called, still marked the indices of consumer buying and selling. Money Supply One, the guardian of the debtor-masses.

Katherine Graham of the Washington Post was linked to Lazard by family, her Blumenthals married into Eugène Meyer's family, forging a connection that gave Graham a close tie to Lazard that lasted all her life. It was she who first set aside a page, then a section, of her paper, to Stock Exchange information. Very soon the TV channels put market data alongside the political news of the day. The world's poor could now follow the fluctuations of the mystical power system – market forces. Only now, market forces were no longer determined by harvests, weather and wars, but by merchant bankers. At the end of the 20th century, 'traders', trading purely in currencies, could be penniless on Monday and billionaires by the end of the week. They would call themselves also, as the earlier generation of the Sect had done, philanthropists.

As banking continued to evolve, mergers and acquisitions came to represent only a small part of the great banks' power. Their strength now lay in the activities of the market. The old guard of independent banks began to disappear. Paine

Webber gone, Dean Witter joined to Morgan Stanley. Now the new masters of the marketplace were Goldman Sachs, Merrill Lynch and the Salomon Brothers – they had evolved, the dinosaurs became extinct.

It was time to be quoted on the Stock Exchange, after all, everything was for sale. Privatisations in London and Paris then Moscow handed to a new breed of 'traders' not only banks but entire national industries.

In order to grasp the implications of the new financial system, and to recognise how it implies a complete re-appraisal of nation, State and trade, it is enough simply to look at what has happened to one private steel company: Mittal Steel.

Mittal Steel from 1989 – 2005: acquisitions and production in millions of tons:

Production under 1 million tons in 1989.

Acquisitions:

Iron and Steel Co (Trinidad and Tobago). Production:	1m
Sibalsa (Mexico):	2m
Sidbec-Dosco (Canada):	3m
Karmet JSG (Kazakhstan)	
Hamburger Stahlwerke (Germany):	5m
Thyssen Duisburg (Germany):	10m

Inland Steel (USA):	12m
Unimetal (France):	18m
Sidex (Romania)	
Annaba (Algeria)	
Iscor (South Africa):	17m
NovaHut (Czech Rep.):	25m
BH Steel (Bosnia)	
Balkan Steel (Macedonia)	
PHS (Poland)	
ISG (USA):	52m

- ISG had been a fusion of: LVT
Bethlehem Steel
Weirton Steel
Georgetown Steel
Trinidad

Human Valin (China):   47m

In 2005 Mittal checked in at
  valuation: 28.1 billion dollars
  production: 49.2 million tons crude steel
  net profit: 3.3 billion dollars
  workforce: 225,000 people

In 2006 Mittal acquired Arcelor
while Arcelor checked in at
  valuation: 32.6 billion dollars
  production: 49.2 million tons crude steel
  net profit: 3.9 billion dollars
  workforce: 96,000 people

Since this rapid absorption by the predator firm implies an uncontrollable logic motivated by men in a state of market hysteria no different from the participants in the gold rushes of the past or the swarms of gold diggers on the muddy gold mountains of Brazil today, the end-game can only be that the world's entire steel output will end up in their hands, and if not theirs, then another's. There is no political system in place to change this situation. Political democracy, of elected Senate or Parliament, was designed to assure that this situation should not be interfered with, for to it, this is the free movement of market forces. This means that political democracy is the obedient servant of the financial oligarchy, a public relations branch of an unelected élite. When the mathematical logic torpedoes the doctrine of unlimited increase, the financial system will sink. 'Democracy' will go down with the ship.

III

The perception that banking practice has in the last third of the last century not only grown and evolved but experienced a change of identity, that is, it has gone from a static fiduciary and advisory position between State and private money to entering the market itself, makes it necessary to perceive that the bankers have changed, this change resulting from new behaviour by the members of the old Banking Houses combined with the admission of a new breed of bankers, inside the great Houses but not linked by blood.

Let this be restated, for from it can be deduced how things are today and what may be expected tomorrow. Banking practice has radically transformed itself until it has become a quite new phenomenon. Bankers are not what or who they were, having in large part participated in the shattering of the Sect as an inherited family élite, interlinked by marriage and inheritance until, with important exceptions, it became an élite linked uniquely by the financial contract, masonic but not freemasonic.

The essential change from old, static wealth to new, mobile wealth can be seen as a logical outcome of the primary Assignat principle. Wealth, or simply financial power was based on net asset value. This situation metamorphosed into one where financial power became the ability to wield or command debt, that is to use it by elimination or decrease, either way to manoeuvre debt. In the first static model ownership of a building. In the second mobile model to raise debt on the building.

It was in the nature of the Sect's first phase of power, based as it was on holding capital and then supervising the capital projects, that money had to be held in the same hands, long-term. As the capital projects burgeoned and moved across frontiers it necessitated that the banker in London had utterly guaranteed links with Hamburg and New York. The Sect from the outcome, once assured by its institutions (banks) and its instruments (Assignats – paper currency – credit facilities), was able to command the Assembly politics of France, America and England. And it was safe in doing this by one simple anthropology, the Banking House was just that, a family house! Therein lay its security and its stability, and in its dynasties lay its statist power, that is to say, its continuity.

The Sect for the very reason of its inner consistency was by that same token destined to submit to change. Its physicality, the actuality of its wealth, guaranteed that it would eventually submit to the inexorable law of events which Napoleon, echoing Voltaire, called 'La Force des Choses'. Born out of a hurricane, the Revolution (the instrument of the Assignat) and its Napoleonic Wars (the institution of the bank as family House), it gathered its increasing strength with each new tempest, American Civil War, Boer War, World War One, Korea, Vietnam, Iraq and Afghanistan. Yet these storms also saw the emergence of a new breed of bankers. The instruments changed their nature entirely, and so did the institutions. The old blood loyalties collapsed before the need to draft in the upstart brokers. Banks closed, merged, were superseded by trading houses. Greed replaced the hard-won social respect that had been so tenaciously fought for, and that greed which seemed to imply limitless increase falling into the hands of a decreasing wealthy élite, inevitably began to indicate a coming and ultimate crash.

Modern banking, for it is nevertheless a medieval institution poised in its earlier phase between merchants and princes, takes its archetypal form from the Frankfurt bankers, Mayer Amschel Bauer and Jacob Schiff. From their double House they indicated their trade with two signs: Zum Roten Schild and Zum Schiff. The former family changed their name to that of their emblematic shield. Rothschild had five sons. He was to set up a pattern that was to be copied by the early banking families and as a result of its success was to define the nature of money's movement across first countries then continents. Of the sons, Amschel was sent to Berlin, Salomon to Vienna, Jacob to Paris, Kalmann to Naples, and Nathan to London.

Just as Rothschild had made his mark as a financial giant following the collapse of the Napoleonic Order in 1815, so the family of the American banker Joseph Seligman emerged on the ruins of a post-bellum USA within hours of General Lee's surrender. Seligman spread out his family on the archetypal model of his famous predecessor. Of the sons, William was sent to Paris, Henry to Frankfurt, Isaac to London, Joseph, James and Jesse were assigned to New York, and Abraham and Leopold were sent to San Francisco. J&W Seligman and Company, World Bankers was born.

In 1867 two American bankers, Kuhn and Loeb, joined up with Jacob Schiff, formerly the Frankfurt neighbour of Rothschild, to form Kuhn, Loeb and Company.

Another key figure in these formative years was Paul Warburg, sent by Rothschilds to join Kuhn, Loeb in 1902. It was he who first proposed the adoption of the Aldrich House to create a Central Bank to serve as a clearing house. In 1913 the Act was passed to create the Federal Reserve System, thus handing over money irrevocably as an index of political power to private banking.

It would be fatally misleading to deduce from these remarkable beginnings a racial programme. It is a politically distorted view of usury finance to lay it at the door of one race. To do so would also fail to understand it in its modern configurations. The ethos that raised Hitler to popular power was a direct product of banking policy towards post-War Germany, devastating the solidity of the Reichsmark, and the ethos that established the regime in a decade of absolute power would have been equally impossible without Hitler's brilliant banker, Schacht, to say nothing of Wall Street's amorous support. Jerusalem has never been the Sect's Holy City, it is not even New York. Perhaps it is Las Vegas, where pilgrims set out daily to hand their wealth over to its banks, and become infected with the fever that inures the citizen to the bitter-sweet truth that they cannot win but the bank goes on.

It has been this continuity due to strict application of the genealogical principle which has not only assured the burgeoning wealth of the Sect, but, more importantly, managed to convince people that that is how things were, that money and wealth were always thus. In other words that the sheer unreality of symbolic money and interest on it was reality itself.

It is by a full understanding of what banking has been that it will become possible to realise that in this time it has changed utterly. It is, therefore, by a full understanding of what bankers were that it will become possible to realise that the human species is now dealing with a quite different animal.

The decision, itself a necessary imposition, by the Sect to maintain both secrecy and continuity, gave birth to the great Banking Houses. In Europe: Rothschild, Sassoon, Cassel, Baring, Calliard, Hirsch, Warburg, Maxim; Bamburg-Ludwig, founder of Deutsche Bank; Heinrich, founder of Paribas; Schiff; Bischoffsheim, General Credit and Finance; Goldschmidt, Société Générale; Casimir Salvador, Crédit Mobilier; Henry Oppenheim; and Seligman.

In the Ottoman Dawlet: Camondo, Société Générale de l'Empire Ottoman; Abraham-Behor, Emile and Isaac Periere, Imperial Ottoman Bank; Allatini, Salonika; Theodore Tubini, Crédit Générale Ottoman, Theodore Baltazzi, Bank of Constantinople; Sassoon; Alfred André, Lons Steeg, Imperial Ottoman Bank (in 1923 Steeg dropped 'Imperial' from the Bank's name); Oppenheim.

In the USA: Seligman, Guggenheim, Belmont, Rothschild, Kuhn, Loeb, Goldman, Sachs, Bronfman, Lazarus Straus, Samuel Lewisohn, Speyer,

Lazarus Hallgarten, Abraham Lehman, Baruch Wertheim, and Rockefeller.

While the bank as family system suited the logic of markets and cash flow it might not have emerged if it had not been for the uncontrolled urge of the bankers themselves to emulate the ruling class in Europe and America. The ruling class in England was an aristocracy, France, land of the Revolution, had seen Napoleon's Empire, Restoration, Napoleonic 'Restoration', Bourbons again, and finally a self-styled Republic that could boast a continuity of power mixing two aristocracies, one historical the other a staged empire. The authentic nature of aristocracy had been land-based, a system that had only survived in England, and with it went its creed, 'Noblesse Oblige!' The aristocracy were the guardians and protectors of their peasants from their point of view. In the view of the lower orders they were their name, they were their title. A name was established by lineage and a title by having a 'place'. When the Conservatives wanted Disraeli to enter the peerage the objection was not that he was jewish but that he did not have a 'place'. "Then get him one," and they did, and he emerged as Lord Beaconsfield. Lineage gave status and it served the spread of interlocking financial instruments. Take the banking family of March, and observe the gain in social status and the expansion from money into markets.

Juan March Ordinas, 1880–1962: Founder of the Groupe. Creation of the Bank March in 1926. Creation of the Foundation March in 1955.

Juan March Servera, 1906–1973: eldest son of founder. Inheritor of Direction of the Groupe in 1962.

Juan March Delgado (1940–): eldest son of March Servera (note adoption of Bourbon principle of same name for first son). Co-President of Groupe March. Co-President of Financial Corporation Alba. President of the Foundation Juan March. Administrator of the Bank March. Administrator of the Foundation Internationale Carrefour.

Carlos March Delgado (1945–): second son of March Servera. Co-President of Groupe March. Co-President of Financial Corporation Alba. President of Bank March. Administrator of Carrefour. Vice-President of the Foundation Juan March.

Juan March de la Lastra (1974–): eldest son of Carlos – named as the Administrator of Bank March.

A genealogical study of the families listed here, far from complete, spanning Europe, USA and the Ottoman Dawlet, would show a pattern of family linkages by marriage so intricate that the final diagram would resemble a map of the London Underground. It may be that it was the practice of dowry and marriage settlement which first opened up to the Sect their own banking practices of merger and acquisition.

In 'The Vanderbilt Era', Louis Auchincloss wrote:

"The new rich of New York in the 1880s were not an aristocracy, nor did they succeed one. America has never had a true aristocracy, unless the old planters of the antebellum South were one. An aristocracy must have its base in the ownership and cultivation of land. The tradesmen and money-lenders of cities, no matter how long established and no matter what their personal dignity or moral code, can never be other than a bourgeoisie, which is why it never takes one class of capitalists very long to amalgamate with another."

If the Sect could not become aristocrats, since they aspired to be them, it was because they were not interested in the land and its inescapable reality, the peasants and farmers. Yet the allure of power and wealth remained their prerogative in style and in life. Civilisation itself. Now the historical aristocracy was broken, first in France then in Germany, and finally in England. If two World Wars had decimated the remaining titles, the post-War settlement systematically and doctrinally abolished the whole class. Death-duties at the level of law and a social ethos that preached anti-elitism as a policy soon laughed off the last aristocratic group still functioning. The abolition of fox-hunting in England was never about the poor fox but was the symbolic end of the gentry, no longer entitled to gallop over farmers' fields. The absolute nature of this social cleansing was seen in the regular inquisition performed on television by talk show and documentary again and again. While the politicians were given free rein to attack the aristocracy, it kept their attention off the financial system which they still little understood, the Sect itself had fixed its greedy eyes on this glamorous theatre. They were, after all, the new power élite. Why should they not be the new aristocracy also?

* * * * *

In order to grasp the situation that now exists it is important to recognise what has already gone.

Hilaire Belloc, the last century's profoundest political theorist, stated it with clarity. He said:

"The old organisation of government by a commanding and an accepted class has gone forever. Nothing has yet taken its place. ... The desire of the bulk for Aristocratic government is clean gone, for good or ill, as a lost religion. With its passing and the passing at the same time of the Aristocratic class belonging to it, the whole nature of the State has suffered transformation."

He was acutely aware that the parliamentary system, the adversarial party system of the French and English 'Revolutions' (1789 and 1688), could not survive.

"The House of Commons is going down into a sort of tomb, wherein survives like a skeleton the ritual alone of what was once living movement and the names alone of what were once actual things. ...

"It is the loss of the desire for Aristocratic government on the part of the mass which has left the House today bereft of moral authority. Even though the House of Commons were to become as clean as it is now corrupt, as nice as it is nasty, as noble as it is now mean and petty, or as dignified as it is now vulgar and contemptible, this factor alone, the loss of the popular desire to be ruled by a few, would be fatal to its continued power."

Belloc wrote that in 1920. He did not then imagine that the old system would be given a final lease of life by the advent of the Second World War which allowed the most gifted of the old regime, single-handedly, to rescue Britain. However, the funeral of Winston Churchill in mid-century can be taken as the definitive end of the Aristocratic epoch. Now at the opening of a new century Britain is governed by canaille, men and women who can barely enunciate let alone construct grammatical sentences, and where one front bench socialist MP not only made three grammatical errors in one sentence, but regularly failed to conjugate appropriately the verb 'to be'.

On the issue of Aristocracy, Belloc is categoric:

"It [Parliament] could only be resurrected with the resurrection of Aristocracy, and the resurrection of Aristocracy, once dead, is a thing unknown in history and impossible to man."

According to Belloc, three hundred years ago a new governing class supplanted the Kings of

England. That class became, in his term, 'sacramental'. He noted:

"It was worshipped. It sought to deserve worship. What had come, in the place of kingship, was an Aristocratic State, a State governed by an Oligarchy indeed, but by an Oligarchy which received the permanent and carefully preserved respect of its fellow-citizens."

Belloc takes the term to be more than its Greek meaning, "but a particular public temper which favours the power of a restricted class. ... Its prime characteristic is that of a permanent (though often vague) body in the State which governs through the moral authority conferred on it by a general respect." One of the major strengths of this system is its unified inner structure: "The Judiciary is not separate from the Legislature, nor the Legislature from the Executive; for all three belong essentially to the Aristocratic body. ... All the activities of the State meet in a common class, the members of which support each other."

He defines two necessary conditions for this system to work: "The desire for Aristocracy in those who accept its rule; a response to this desire in those who exercise that rule."

The character which is needed to sustain the Aristocratic body is firstly, dignity. The second, closely allied to dignity is a readiness in the individual to sacrifice himself for the good of the whole.

Belloc explains: "...it is in the Aristocratic spirit that a member of the government caught taking a bribe, or telling a public lie, should resign: and until quite lately [1920!] such resignations were the rule." To this he adds a subtle element which is what he defines as "the representative character of the Aristocrat properly so called." That is to say that while he maintains a superior and aloof distinction from the masses, yet at the same time he must be national: "...he must so act that the less fortunate man reveres him as a sort of glorified example of himself. A living Aristocracy is always very careful to be in communion with, actually mixed with, the mass of which it is itself the chief. It has an unfailing *flair* for national tradition, national custom, and the real national will."

Noting that "wealth, position through wealth, the digestion of new wealth" are native to a governing aristocracy, he allows this as part of a greater whole, but insists: "When the attitude towards wealth becomes at once a principle thing and *an isolated thing* it is a proof, and a cause of, disintegration in the governing class." From this summary of the Bellocian position it follows firstly that there is now no active Aristocracy and secondly that governance is no longer in the hands of a body respected by the masses.

So it has been, that as governance by a superior group bonded to service and to a high morality worthy of respect has disappeared, that a new class has emerged. The new class being the holders of wealth, are by that token, the holders of power. What, then, has been their social practice and persona? Most importantly the first assessment has to take into account the new situation defined previously, that banking, financial services and institutions have merged into one evolved élite with commodities and communications owner-ship. What is revealed when the new power élite are put under the arc-lights of critical analysis?

It was the fantasy of the Sect that they would turn into the Second Estate, in other words, with christianity abolished through the invention of the Secular State the role of the clergy fell vacant. What was required by the State system was a replacement for monastic banking, for Richelieu and Mazarin. This became the passionate ambition of the first modern bankers, that is, that they would be accepted as servants of the Princes and Kings, gain status and recognition, win access then social initiation, titles and honours and at last, 'a place'. Marxist analysts of brilliance like Pinçon and Pinçon-Charlot have measured the Sect as pertaining to the bourgeoisie. They see their wealth as simply alongside the bourgeois wealth of industry and mining. This view, while yielding unnerving insights, seems to fail in its inability to recognise the urgent transformative and bulimic nature of the wealth system today.

The dynamic of wealth systems, active and evolutionary, must be seen in relation to social systems, passive and devolutionary. The first stage of the affair is the direct result of the French Revolution. The immediate effect of this bloody upheaval was the rupture of the old society (Ancien Régime) and the re-stratification caused by parliamentism (lawyer class). The shattering of the Aristocratic system did not, however, leave a void. The Terror and the new financial order both removed a system of inherited wealth and emptied the chateaux. The motor of the Revolution was still running. Napoleon's Empire created, as it were, a new aristocracy. The Louis XVIII restoration was not a continuity of Bourbon power but a concordance with the Revolution. The rule had gone from the monarch to the Assembly (the politico-legalists) and the money had gone from the Clergy to the Sect. The Metternich Settlement was not a monarchist counter-revolution, it was a bitter reformist solution. Titles that once went with land now went with money. Louis XVIII took the throne of France in 1815. In 1818 Nathan Rothschild gathered the 240 million francs owed in reparations to Russia, Prussia and England. He became indispensable to the Finance Ministers of the King. In 1817 Metternich raised the Austrian Rothschilds to the titular nobility for their help in handling Austria's claims on France due to the war. In 1822 the five brothers received the hereditary title of Baron. In 1823 James Rothschild was made Chevalier de la Legion d'Honneur, then Officer. In 1829 he joined the Aristocratic 'Cercle de l'Union' and later the Jockey Club, where his son Alphonse was co-opted in 1852 after being black-balled twice. Alphonse also became Director of the Bank of France, as did his son, Edouard. Lionel's son, Nathaniel, was elevated to the peerage by Queen Victoria in 1885.

What is witnessed, but not grasped, in these transformations is the end of one social system and a quite new one that in its later phase will not even necessitate the forms of acceptance once so important. In it people are so busy enviously watching the 'new rich' become integrated into the élite that they fail to see the end of an age.

In order that the Sect should triumph, not only by becoming the Second Estate but the First, the abolition of the old order is needed to make way for the new. So it was that, taking advantage of two World Wars, the financial sector (the Sect) was able to exploit the poetic dreams of equality engendered by the levelling of the masses in the genocidal trench warfare, and to tell the survivors that the living should abolish hereditary privilege. As a result the twentieth century saw an ongoing series of legal judgments deliberately aimed at the levelling of the old Aristocracy. Death duties were the principal weapons of destruction, followed by the pressure to break up the great estates of the gentry. 'Legislated Bankruptcy' as it was defined by an English Earl. A further important instrument of change was the virtual prevention of ennoblement by the monarchy. In England the comic invention of 'Life Peers' appointed to the House by politicians was accompanied by the helpless inability of the monarch to create the higher titles of Earl, Marquis and Duke. The English Aristocratic rule that had sustained and preserved England since Henry VIII created it to replace the ruined Plantagenet legitimacy, using the superbly acquired monastery wealth, was being wound down.

Along with the specific legislation carrying financial sanction came a persistent and persuasive indoctrination that told the masses that the House of Lords should be abolished since, "Men should not be set up to govern others just because of the accident of birth." The argument was always presented with that lethal mixture of passion appealing to reason. Of course it was spurious. There is absolutely nothing accidental about a birth, indeed legitimacy had been the foundation of the State. The great traumata of English history had been the usurpation of the Plantagenet inheritance and the exiling of the Stuart legitimacy. Election by a universal suffrage through a party system of men of dubious background funded by trade unions, industry and high finance, the most manipulable of methods, is mathematically bound to be a result of chance. In order to re-assure the public that this great levelling was 'a good thing', the bankers devised a scheme which indicated that the Aristocratic heritage would pass to the people: a National Trust was set up to acquire the stately homes of England. Within a couple of decades the Sect were themselves confident enough to abandon secrecy and openly buy the great Palaces. The great unobserved leveraged buy-out.

So it was that while the old élite were being shunted into the siding of television serials and documentaries, the new élite were puffing into the station of events. Their method had been that of the cuckoo in the nest. The christian nobility had title, genealogical integrity, and a semiotic system of heraldry which to enter falsely in the past led to beheadings. That was not aesthetics taken to extremes. Heraldry was a systematic record of legitimate lineage and union, with the halving and quartering of arms. Bauer and Seligman, as already noted, had adopted their shop signs as crests. Then it was that Bauer changed his name to the name of his logo, as it were. He became, comically, Mister Red Shield, as if Prince Charles should call himself Prince Three White Feathers. First name, then titles, and then the genealogy. The construction of a family tree demands two practices. The continuity of a hereditary line, father to son, and the binding-in of possible spread through marrying out, firstly through intermarriage, cousin to cousin and eventually by easing the rules to let other members of the Sect join wealth to blood. The Rothschild control over family marriages in the first few generations was a deliberate and calculated re-enactment of the European practice recorded in the Almanach de Gotha, a directory immediately banned by the Allied Command after World War Two, only much later to emerge with all its 'new' names. The marriage chart of the Rothschilds is identical in principle and method to the monitored policy of Queen Victoria, herself a bastard, which tied the whole of Europe in a monarchic unity. That unity was finally to be shattered in 1914 by the Hapsburgs, who in the end yielded to an illegitimate union, which in turn resulted in the destruction of the whole monarchic system, bringing down Austria, Germany, Russia, Turkey, along with a time-limit set on England.

If, as now seems convincing, Ernst Nolte's view of one European Civil War stretching from 1914 to 1945, in effect a Second Thirty Years War, is accepted, then it provides a perfect time-frame within which the Sect could effectively take control of the political system that had not only failed but somnambulistically allowed that War to take place. By the end of that century the social landscape was able to reveal that power had passed to a new class openly in command. The Sect had started in its archetypal Rothschild pattern from 1815 to 1915. From the Korean War to the Iraqi and Afghan invasions can be observed and recorded the new burgeoning-in-wealth and decreasing-in-membership of a ruthless and globe destroying élite before whom the world may well tremble, although it scarcely knows their names. They are the same people who over the last few decades have systematically bought up the historical castles and palaces of Europe, and for more fun, built new ones, world-wide.

IV

Marxism viewed from the ruins of the Soviet Union can now only attract the quixotic few. Nevertheless its distortion and obscuring of social processes reached into every sphere of intellectual activity during the twentieth century. Many theorists who would have been shocked at the name of marxist still approached the subject with, at the least, a background wash of communist colouring. The three doctrines of what Koestler named 'The God that Failed', marxism, have all proved unsustainable when tested against events.

Firstly, Marx's sanctioning the procedures of usury under the blanket doctrine of surplus-value is no longer shocking now that his financial subsidies from the Rothschilds are common knowledge. Although ferociously anti-semitic, Marx became the protector of banking.

Secondly, the doctrine of dialectical-materialism as a dynamic to deal with any social process, thesis-antithesis-synthesis, proved to have failed disastrously when the full extent of Stalin's genocidal dictatorship was exposed. The Central Committee's 'explanation' of having succumbed to 'the Cult of Personality' did not wash, since 'personality' was a Hegelian concept that could not be subsumed under materialist philosophy. Sartre saw this only to find that his attempt at rescue was haughtily dismissed.

Thirdly, and perhaps most remarkably, the system was purportedly based on tracing all historical events to social causes, yet marxism failed to construct a viable and critical phenomenology of power and the state. With the marxist empire shattered, and that, not by nuclear weaponry but by the applied surplus-value technologies of the bankers, it cannot but be noted that in the monoculture of capitalism today, these three 'failures' are still the common coin of what passes for political discourse. The new high-capitalism which is the hegemonic and logical unification of wealth systems, is still criticised from an antiquated 'leftist', in America 'liberal' position, using an arsenal of out-dated slogans and arguments. This suits the new power élite, for it means anti-globalism can be de-activated by the same means that had been so successful against the massively structured Soviet State.

It is the matter of this third 'failure' that must be over-passed. Its subject is also that active and influencing zone in which the 'personalities' inside events behave – a behaviour at once intensely personal and dynamically political. In around the middle of the last century, the present author was approached by Princess Marthe Bibesco to make an English adaptation of a play she had written. Its subject was Stalin's mother, and the play drama-tised her struggle to convince her son that even residence in the Kremlin did not assure his absolute rule. In order to rule Russia, she insisted, Stalin had to sleep in the bed of Catherine the Great. The theme was given its existential power by the writer's own struggle to be a chatelaine. In her own life, as a Rumanian exile in France, she had succeeded in ousting the great Colette, then the Baronne de Jouvenal des Ursins, from her magnificent Chateau de Castel-Novel, only to fail in her campaign to be the new Baronne after Colette's divorce. In its day, Bibesco's theme appeared subjective and scarcely serious as politics. Only Camus seemed to suggest that people activated events, while Malraux convinced the body of writers in his time to follow the materialist view that events made men.

With a different perspective it is possible to trace patterns and connections, and it is these which enlace people to events. Follow the trail. Bibesco wanted to be 'castled', and her adultery with the Baron drove the rejected Colette into the arms of her husband's son by his first marriage, Bertrand de Jouvenal. In this two-year love affair Colette liberated Bertrand from the strictures of the Jouvenals and opened to him her world of immediacy, taste and freedom. Without this life-initiation Bertrand would never have written the great text for which he is today renowned, 'Du Pouvoir'. Bibesco's play was able to express her own theme to perfection. In the palace that was once the seat of power of Catherine the Great, an Orthodox seminarist turned revolutionary had bloodily taken over from his Leader, Lenin, and now held the titular position, but the parvenu never truly arrives. Bibesco's central perception was profoundly true. The locus of power, precisely down to the very bed, is the proof and evidence desired by legitimate power and required by usurped power. Sultan Abdulhamid II refused to sleep in Dolmabache Palace, designed by Europeans to replace Topkapi Village-as-Palace from where the Osmanli Dawlet had governed for centuries. Dolmabache was Palace as centralist-base of the kingdom. It had been invented in the age that had abolished kingship, beheaded the King and made a museum of Versailles. Sultan Abdulhamid II built Yildiz Palace which, as a set of Kiosks, represented his determination to de-centralise State power and move back to the minimalist rule that had epitomised Osmanli governance. After the Kemalist coup d'état, Kemal could not wait to occupy the Palace of the Sultans, and passed his final drunken days in Dolmabache guarded by his inner sodomite circle, Nuri Conker, Salih Bozok, Kiliç Ali and Recep Zühtü, at least according to his admiring biographer, H.C. Armstrong, and his envious biographer, Patrick Kinross.

The reason the Revolutionary or Coup Leader fails seems to have two elements. The personal occupation of the power zone is not enough.

Lacking is the right to be there and lacking is the social dynamic that was sustained by the legitimate ruler.

A phenomenological study of power indicates that the castle, the chateau or palace, and the great houses of Europe, represent the unique zone and epicentre from which issue both policy and programme. Simon Thurley in 'The Royal Palaces of Tudor England' puts it thus: "The houses of the Kings and Queens of England up to the eighteenth century were far more than residences, they were centres of power, the hub of the country's interests, hopes and aims, all of which focussed on an individual – the monarch. From earliest times royal houses were built to accommodate the liturgy of monarchy." Thurley observes that under the Plantagenet Kings the King's Domus or household numbered around 100 and moved easily across the kingdom from house to house. From 100 to 150 in 1100, it grew to around 500 by 1300. As Treasury, Exchequer and Chancery were moved out from the King's presence to Westminster, this both set up structural government and at the same time gave the seat of government as the key locus of the King, his 'Palatium', his palace, his seat of power.

In 1413 Henry V selected Sheen to be the seat of his dynastic residence. The Lancastrian House had usurped the Plantagenet legitimacy, and as a result the Crown under his father Henry IV had not succeeded in imposing itself on the nobles and nation merely by the fact of conquering then killing the rightful monarch, Richard II. Stemming from this very insecurity, Henry V felt compelled to secure his castle.

Thurley observes: "Unlike previous royal houses there was a physical barrier between the accommodation of the monarch and that of the Court. A moat divided the lodges of the King and Queen from the remainder of the house. ... What Sheen provided was a potential for privacy within the main building and, more important, a bid for the legitimacy of privacy for a monarch. Kings of England began to place more and more barriers, both physical and organisational, between themselves and their courtiers."

Thurley gives two proofs of the political philosophy underlying the need for monarchy to mount a stage of magnificence before the people. Sir John Fortescue in his 'The Governance of England': "Item, it shall nede that the kyng haue such tresour, as he mey make new bildynges whan

213

he woll, ffor his pleasure and magnificence: and as he mey bie hym riche clothes, rich furres. ... riche stones ... and other juels and ornamentes conuenyent to his estate roiall. And often tymes he woll bie riche hangynges and other apparell ffor his howses. ... ffor yff a king did not so, hor myght do, he lyved then not like his estate, but rather in miserie, and in more subgeccion than doth a priuate person."

In 'La Toison d'or' (c. 1470) Guillaume Fillastre, Chancellor of the Burgundian Order of the Golden Fleece, stated that the chief virtue of a Prince was magnificence. These sums were spent "not upon himself but upon public objects." The poet, John Skelton, believed that "magnificence signified the physical expression of power by properly measured liberality in all things." In Thurley's summing-up of the balanced view of that time, he goes on to note that Sir John Fortescue's criticism of Henry VI was his "grete pouertie" and his reluctance to keep a "worshipful and grete household." This was seen as one of his worst flaws and one of the causes of his downfall and a madness, fuelled by the guilt of usurpation, that led to the Wars of the Roses.

The outcome of that disastrous event – which Shakespeare saw as the whole arena of power politics in which usurpation is the ultimate civic crime and the door to anarchy – was the triumph of the House of Tudor but the end of the Plantagenet dynasty. So it was that the great 105 year rule of the Tudors, which was to be the glory of English history, was born out of the double trauma of usurpation, the killing of Richard II and later of Richard III.

The first of the usurping Tudors, Henry VII, directing the completion of his new chapel at Westminster, ordered that it be painted with "our arms, badges, cognisants, and other convenient painting, because such decoration to a King's work appertaineth."

The castle, therefore, was the public showing forth of kingship and by the same token was a fountain of hospitality and largesse. This was a generosity never reserved for the Royal Host, nor even by extension, for the Royal Court. Its largesse spilled out to feed the people. On a Royal Progress, or a Royal Staying, wine flowed, feasts were shared and coin was scattered.

John Skelton's counsel to his royal pupil was "Be bountiful, liberal and lavish." Henry VIII took it to heart. Erasmus considered Henry "the man most full of heart" and "a universal genius". Thomas More said of him: "The King's Majesty has more learning than any English monarch possessed before him." He had a passion for astronomy and his own astrolabe was made by Sébastian le Senay. As a cartographer he had a now famous collection of thirty five maps which hung in his Palace of Whitehall. Henry was one of the founders of the English Navy, which at his ascension was but a few ships and by the end of his reign stood at 46 warships, 13 galleys, with 26 other ships purchased and 13 captured. He was the virtual initiator of the now standard and necessary Summit Conference, that political institution which more than any other proves the mythic nature of democratic decision-making. His greatest political achievement was in activating his perception that the Roman Church's power lay not in its theology but in the Papacy. His statal break with Rome was the Reformation itself, not the sacramental debate. He had done what neither Garibaldi nor Mussolini ever dared to complete. Not until the 21st century with Professor Gardner's monumental study 'The King's Reformation' has Henry's genius been acknowledged. The phenomenology of Henrician rule is to be identified with his transformation of Cardinal Wolsey's Palace at Hampton Court along with the great houses across his kingdom, the stopping-places of his Royal Progresses which unified the nation.

Significantly the history of Hampton Court spreads out the whole political reality that is here being claimed for the importance and meaning of the castle. It had been created by Wolsey on a house previously owned by Lord Daubeny. In 1515 Wolsey had been made Cardinal. Edward Hall's 'Triumphant Reign of King Henry the Eighth' (1547) records that "the King took his Progress westwards, and visited his towns and castles there and heard the complaints of his poor commons; and always, as he rode, he hunted and liberally gave away the venison. And in the middle of September, he came to his manor of Woking." There he met up with his new Cardinal who was busily engaged in the building of his new Palace.

On 29 October 1515, the King attended the launch of the enormous 'Virgin Mary', a ship of nearly 800 tons, with 120 oars, 207 guns, and able to carry 1,000 men. Henry piloted the ship down the Thames.

On 22 December 1515, the King appointed Wolsey Lord Chancellor and handed over to him the Great Seal of England. The activation of Hampton Court as the Chancellor's headquarters and seat of power marked it out as a new kind of Palace. The King's former tutor, John Skelton, saw that the wielding of the wealth, which IS substantive power, was in the hands of the Chancellor, and his Palace was the proof. So he let loose his famous attack:

"Why come ye not to Court?
To the King's Court or to Hampton Court?
The King's Court should have the precedence,
But Hampton Court hath the pre-eminence."

Wolsey ordered Skelton's arrest but he sought sanctuary in Westminster Abbey. The flowering of Henry's political activity attuned to the influence of Anne Boleyn also made him aware of Wolsey as over-reacher. Firstly, challenged by Wolsey's attraction to power, he decided to take Hampton Court from him on 2 January, 1529. Secondly, following the crisis of discovering Boleyn's adultery allied to her own over-reaching, he at last recognised Hampton Court's meaning.

Simon Thurley writes in his history, 'Hampton Court':

"The birth of Edward VI in the Queen's Bedchamber on 12 October, St. Edward's Day, can be counted as one of the most important events in the Palace's history. Not only was it the fulfilment of the King's most fervent wish; it was the fulfilment of his purpose for Hampton Court as conceived during 1537."

From then until the end of his reign Hampton Court is one of the dominant zones of his Regal Progresses and stays. In 1539 an Act of Parliament was passed decreeing that "an honour would be created, centred on it," that is, a group of manors held by one Lord, thus the Honour of Hampton Court was a collection of royal property holdings based on and around Hampton Court. A programme was begun to acquire tens of thousands of acres in Surrey and Middlesex. It also set up a chase, a private forest or a zone defined as a royal game reserve. The Chase was defined in the Act of Parliament to be for forestry and hunting. In the end it was not only forest but 10,000 acres of parkland taking in manor houses and parishes. The Palace became the most splendid setting for his royal hospitality and that meant the place appointed to receive important foreign visitors. In 1546 from June to September, the Palace was adorned with tents and pavilions, and superb, solid banqueting halls to receive the guests. The occasion was the reception in honour of France's Admiral Claude d'Annebault who had come to ratify the Treaty between France and England. On August 23 the Admiral and his 200-strong entourage was met three miles from the Palace by the ten-year-old Prince Edward surrounded by eighty English Lords and gentlemen in golden livery, who escorted him to the Palace. The Treaty was signed in the Chapel Royal.

It has been part of the intense and devoted iconoclasm of monarchy that has persisted in sustaining the quite mythical view of Henry as a monster of cruelty and self-indulgence who somehow held the throne of England for over 36 years while uniquely obsessed with his six wives. He liberated England from the anti-intellectual tyranny of Papism and, educated by Erasmus, created the foundations of a modern State. His dynasty was to last over 100 years. It took three Tudor monarchs to complete the convulsions of the State's escape from the darkness of Rome, and the extended tortures of it saw the regicide and rejection of the Stuarts, which gave evidence enough that without Henry's ruthless abolition of monasticism, modern England could not have emerged.

These tremendous events in the life of England's greatest King centre on Hampton Court, in a saga which significantly begins with the expulsion of the Financier-Cardinal and the taking of monarchic power in the acquired ownership of that Palace.

It was in the nature of Henry's renowned largesse that at Hampton Court he used the function of the Great Hall for big receptions. It was in his nation-wide programme of building royal residences that he re-configured Palace as country house. Throughout his reign he maintained this connection of the table uniting Court and people. The Lord Steward was in charge of nineteen offices including the bakehouse, pantry, cellar, butchery, pitcher-house, spicery, chaundry, ewrye, boiling-house, larder, accatary, poultry, scalding-house, squillery, pastry, waffrey, confectary, woodyard and the great kitchen itself.

In 1526 around 600 people were entitled to eat in the hall and outer rooms. 230 domestic servants would be fed elsewhere. At a nearby house meals would have been prepared for a further 800 people. All this was apart from the King's table which would on occasion seat the highest noblemen. The Eltham Ordinances decreed that

"Hall should be kept at the greater houses." Royal parks provided 600 head of venison for the Royal Household. When Henry VIII died he possessed over 60 houses, mostly built by himself. These houses were to form the nexus of aristocratic country residences which would permit the gentry to govern Britain over five centuries. In Harrison's 'Description of England' he states that Queen Elizabeth I's policy was that: "Everie noble man's house is hir Palace." The social fabric was tightly woven into one, monarchy, aristocracy, the people. From this pattern came the popular folk saying that "an Englishman's home is his castle." During Henry's reign he made 1,150 moves between houses with his Court. 830 of these were to his own houses. At his accession there were 45 hereditary peers: one duke, one marquess, twelve earls and thirty-one barons. Between them they owned up to 70% of England. Henry was to create 37 peers. He reigned for 37 years. During that time he re-distributed large tracts of liberated monastic lands to his nobles. His legacy was not, after all, a dynasty but an educated and experienced social élite who took up office during the reign of his daughter Elizabeth. With the Cecils at their head the country was to be under aristocratic rule up to the death of Churchill in mid-twentieth century, and when the time came to abolish the hereditary peerage it was Lord Cranbourne, a Cecil, who oversaw the affair at century's end.

In the Black Book it records that in 1472, Edward IV, on Christmas Day at Eltham fed over 2,000 people from his kitchens. Paul Morand in his Journals told of a local lady in her castle in the French countryside who, after the Second World War, still continued her family's tradition of feeding the local villagers and farmers. Morand noted that it would never have occurred to her that entertaining would not include the whole surrounding countryside. Noblesse oblige! Power governance, social connectedness, hospitality, networked centres of residence and rule, this was the organically unified State on which a civilisation came into being, and with its demise that same civilisation – which had been that – totally collapsed. As Belloc observed – only the names remained.

There is now a market of chateaux. This is more than saying that chateaux are on the market. Before, chateaux were rarely sold but rather were conserved. The path from inherited ownership led to State guardianship. Saying that there is a market of chateaux indicates that there is already turnover. In other words, there is already an 'old' generation of 'new rich', who at 50-60 years are selling up. The demand is superior to the offers, that means a flourishing wealth élite. Wealth flows upwards, only the trickle drips down on the increasing masses of the poor.

In the evolutionary phase of the power system a gradual concordance could be observed, firstly with the Sect coming alongside aristocratic and monarchic power, and then secondly, the gradual merging of the two groupings by marriages and financial mergers. The climactic moment could be exemplified by the Lazard Bank's submission to the expanding presence of 'market forces', marked by both the entering of the market, via mergers and acquisitions, that is passing from passive and capital based finance to active fiduciary projects, and by the taking into the Sect of a new aggressive and greedy class of arrivistes. At this stage, in their desperate struggle to survive almost uniquely by the genealogical principle, and by their acquiring the same overt greed as the new money people, came the utter demise of the aristocratic remnant. All social obligation and all civic concern abandoned, it had become inevitable. Following the Bellocian critique, once the collapse has occurred, that aristocratic class is historically irrecoverable.

Society has moved a long way from that social distinction that tried to keep aristocracy apart from wealth as when Kaiser Wilhelm's sister, Princess Hohenzollern, to her confusion found herself seated at dinner next to Cartier, the jeweller. Utterly at a loss to know how to deal with it, the Princess removed her pearls and dropped them on his plate, saying, "Perhaps you could evaluate these for me."

What had once been the tension between aristocracy and wealth slithered down both in style and definition as the tension became that between 'old money' and 'new money', exemplified by Mrs Astor's haughty objection to having America's leading carpet manufacturer to dinner: "Just because I walk on his carpets does not mean he has to sit at my table."

By the end of the Twentieth Century the mere badges of excessive consumption had become the passport to the new power élite. At the funeral of the murdered banker, Safra, in Monte Carlo, one could see France's leading film actor, the Chief Rabbi of Paris, a former Secretary General of the United Nations, and a European Commissioner, alongside other bankers.

As eagerly as the wealthy industrialists and bankers once sought to possess titles, honours and social privileges of access, today they seek to possess the chateau, the yacht, the vineyard, the art-work and the hunting forest. Their activity is making wealth, on occasion and not infrequently, ex nihilo. Their contribution to society is also nil. With their wealth they amass their property: tableaux, bateaux, chateaux.

It is possible simply by tracing the names and backgrounds of the chatelains of the great houses to find one is examining a detailed economic model of a financial thus social devolution. It could be said to represent a shadow stock exchange, and by that same token to be the evidence of a profound change in the power élite, so absolute that it has left virtually no more than an echo of past names.

Three categories – three stages of the end of an age.

One: The Legitimate Chatelain possessing castle, estates and historical title.

Brissac: the chateau above the River Aubance in Anjou is a living evidence of the beauty in disorder of a house built from 15th century towers which grew into a 17th century castle, which in turn was modernised over the coming centuries. The Cosse-Brissac family bought the property in the sixteenth century and today its chatelain is the present Duc de Brissac.

Two: 'The New Legitimacy' of bought or acquired title and the purchase of estate and castle or the building of a new palace. This is the epoch dominated by the Rothschilds, who gave their name to its style – a hideous conglomeration of bought furniture of mixed epochs against a vulgar background of green damasks and scarlet silks. Instant historicity through commissioned portraits by Ingres and Ary Scheffer.

Chateau de Champs: acquired by le Comte Louis Cahen d'Anvers, né Cohen, banker, in 1895. Donated by his son, Charles, to the State in 1934. In 1995 the site of a son-et-lumière spectacle.

In the second category can be identified the arrival of the Sect, and at the same time an important phenomenon of change – the gradual vanishing of many of the great aristocratic families, dying out or falling into poverty alongside a climbing into place of lesser and dubious titles now able to buy up a castle with a history. To this last group their lowly title slides alongside the noble history of the newly acquired house so that only the few will realise that in this lies no continuity. The castle in its origin may have belonged to Gilles de Rais but today there can be staged the social life of the new rich playing at aristocrats, utterly devoid of the duties and obligations of genuine nobility. Even those great families that have maintained their properties over centuries, it must be recognised, are nothing to do with their renowned ancestors. A man who risked his life and wealth to save Marie-Antoinette has little to do with a descendant who lives off son-et-lumière spectacles and tourism. Only the name remains, as Belloc insisted.

Three: The New Order. Now the dominant social ethos is utterly in the hands of the ex-nihilo billionaires, a mixed bag: their revered old guard who prised open the old wealth system, the Lazards, the Rothschilds, the Camondo; then the arrivistes who had arrived, the 'international set', a mixed bag of yankee white trash, jewish and atheist, Russian oligarchs, and the euro-stars – the Pinaults, the Agnellis, the Dessaults, Soros and so on.

It comes as rather a relief to see that in the new category of super-rich, the media celebrities, the film producer-director, Luc Besson, has bought the perfect jewel, Le Chateau de la Trinité-des-Laitiers in Normandy, and turned it into both a residence and a high-tech film factory serving as an Audio Post-Production Facility.

Of the aristocracy, and their relation to the Sect, their devolution can be defined through the three phases outlined above as:

First Stage – they would not sit at table with them.
Second Stage – they got into bed with them.
Third Stage – they had become 'them' – only the name remained.

Stendhal, in his 'Life of Napoleon', wrote:

"Today, in 1837, the peasants and the masses of all the civilised countries of Europe have at last understood that the French Revolution has made them proprietors, and it was Napoleon who taught them this."

This has been the legend of a hyper-capitalism that has turned the Napoleonic modern pyramidic State from a political entity into a financial one, in the process systematically destroying the world's eco-structure and, with mathematical inexorability, reducing the masses of the world to a statistically increasing community of slavery while at the same time elevating an ever-diminishing and tiny élite to an ever-increasing super-wealth, such as history has never recorded before. The 2006 World Wealth Report of Cap-Gemini and Merrill Lynch specifies a mere 78,000 'ultra-rich' defined as possessing 30 million US dollars in liquidity.

Stendhal, like all those infatuated with the undoubted genius of Napoleon, was blinded to the man's character. Napoleon at least was honest about his own ambition and intention. He openly declared his philosophy.

He said: "Every Revolution is a transfer of property."

V

The possessors of the chateaux are by definition the masters. The break with the past, the dysjunction, has, however, created a different role for the new masters, or rather, they have abrogated that particular role which assures coherence to the whole body politic. The Pinçons in their extensive sociological surveys have demonstrated this with inexorable clarity. Calling the new proprietors of the castles the 'neo-chatelains', they explain: "They do not have the same connection to their castle as that of hereditary families. Formerly, when you acquired a chateau you also bought the adjoining agricultural lands and forests. To be a chatelain it was necessary to run a domain that produced benefit. Today, the chateau is sold with, at best, an adjoining park. The new proprietors consider their domain to be a country residence: their children will not have grown up there, nor constructed their memories there. This will make them more liable to sell, which will increase the market."

Tocqueville confirmed the status of the legitimate chatelains: "In the former feudal society, if the lord possessed great rights, he also had great responsibilities."

It is in the incapacity to fulfil 'the great responsibilities' that the downfall of the present power system's social order is assured. The Pinçons, in confirming the nature of the present wealth élite as being without linkage to the surrounding members of the species, allow one to deduce from this a moral evaluation. Earlier finance can be defined as distributive. Modern finance is acquisitive. What was once basically a sharing of provision becomes a refusal to participate in the social nexus. This results in a society that can only view the masses through the distancing and alienating lens of charity.

The Pinçon critique goes more deeply into the social phenomenon of the ultra-rich. They view them not just as the extravagant star individuals of 'tableaux, bateaux, chateaux' but as a class, well aware that it risks at any moment being under siege, which closes ranks both against the outside world and among each other as a unified entity, a separate élite.

In 'Sociologie de la Bourgeoisie' the Pinçons define it thus: "Economic capital, social capital and cultural capital form one system. ... The fortune, the culture, the relations have a symbolic dimension. It is imposed on them to possess societies, lands, domains and residences, to have attended a top school. ... The bourgeoisie need, more than any other class, 'rites of institution'. The (ultra-rich) person must be certified as such, in his totality. The qualities are not separable one from another, it is the combination which makes for excellence. It is to be seen in the scholarly titles, the decorations, the nominations, the annual directories which confirm group membership. Each time, to belong to the list of the elect is to be instituted, as an individual, to be separately, the member of a whole."

This critique goes much further than a Veblen-style categorisation of the wealthy class, noting that "a 'grand bourgeois' cannot be reduced to the definition of his professional activity, since in any event he will have several. He may be a general in the army, or head of a commercial organisation, academician or in agriculture. Of course his real social position results from his profession, but it is also due to the strict ties he has with his equals who occupy the other socially dominant positions. In other words, a grand bourgeois is one by virtue of that system of relations which involve him in the connections appropriate to his milieu."

There follows the devastating social corollary made by the Pinçons: "A worker, even isolated and self-reliant, remains a worker. A 'grand bourgeois' cannot be one all alone. His power is not individual but collective. It is his social class which assures his dominant position. To be a cleaning woman does not require membership of a group. One cannot be one of the 'grande bourgeoisie' without an intense social life."

If one removes the marxist term 'haut bourgeois' since it could imply a marxist solution – the workers unite and disinherit the chatelains – and prefers the term 'ultra-rich', confirming them not just as rich but belonging to the meta-morphosed and modern version of the Sect, then it is possible to arrive at a recognition of just who these ultra-rich are. No, they are not just jews, not freemasons, and not even Americans. They are today's inheritors of that Revolutionary élite, born out of genocide and paper money, and installed in power through a pyramidic State system designed by the Revolution's guardian, Napoleon. After him the struggle was to find a mechanism that would maintain the Revolutionary élite in power. Mao had confirmed that the completion of the Jacobin doctrine lay in the principle of perpetual revolution. That principle turned out to be the application of a dual system. The first element was the universal application of political democracy in its multi-party form. The second element was the interdiction of government to interfere with the market, 'market' being the coded term for the wealth-system based on mathematical instruments tied to a credit practice based in turn on increase in the transaction, that is, usury. Mao's perpetual revolution is that model, in its most refined mode, which is now being imposed with ferocious savagery as the mono-doctrine for the world today. Any State resisting it is in line for 'regime change', any group opposing it is labelled 'terrorist'. Thus following this political programme to its successful conclusion would imply a world state system with its masses pinned in helpless submission to a political class chosen and groomed not to question this underlying world-view. In it war is transformed, as Jünger foretold, into a peace-keeping operation. The financial system, outside any political jurisdiction, is not to be impinged upon by political projects or controls. Errors, when perceived in its system, must be categorised as aberations of a flawless and constant reality which can only be marred by individual acts that while shameful can be punished by handing over the culprit to the judiciary. Corruption – in a multi-national corporation or a third-world (pre-democratic, usually) regime – is a personal sin not a structural flaw.

Yet even supposing that the high-capitalist ethos could continue as it is now, and not collapse, as it inevitably must, as the rich get less and richer while the poor get more and poorer, there is another flaw in the system that no financial manipulation could rescue, should it emerge.

What is the ultimate crack in the golden bowl of the current world system of property and power? It is the human creature it throws up to govern, legislate and enslave its own species while keeping from them the world's wealth. The Sect itself, the moneyed élite and the political class it has set up by the lottery of a mass franchise under the screening of its own experts, is doomed by an inadequacy, moral, spiritual, social and genetic. The Sectarian, ultra-rich, high bourgeois, call him as you may, is the commanding Master, and the Politician, president, prime minister, king, call him as you may, is the obedient slave. In reality the function of today's politician is not to govern – he has no money except the pittance taken in taxation – his role is to distract the masses from the wealth-élite, at best to stop an uprising, at worst to stop a bullet. He is there to assure continuity, to prevent history. Together, these two groups form one brotherhood that represents the power élite. Napoleon had learned that prestige and the symbols of power can hold the political class in total subservience. Having only the trappings and titles of power they long for recognition – 'to be installed'. The Legion of Honour chosen to mark out the State's recognition results in permitting the recipient to wear a five centimetre red ribbon on the breast. The author once asked France's most renowned and loved popular singer, Edith Piaf, why she did not have the Legion d'Honneur. "Because you have to ask for it. Say you would accept it. I could never do that." The politicians, however, must, and do.

The doctrine which underlies the system is that, arrived at from a primal cause, the ultimate purpose for mankind is as follows: Man as a social animal, once free of blood ties, family and tribe, was forced to find a method of living together with his kind. The struggle to arrive at a social model that could let man live forever in peace and harmony with his neighbour, each equal and free, has taken centuries of failed projects, punctuated by terrible wars, famines and disease. Finally, as it were, thanks to the convulsion of the American settlers and the French citizens, after the Americans had slaughtered the Indians and the French the Vendéens, they at last evolved a means of living in perpetual peace. The end was in sight. All that was required now was to impose this system on a resistant and aggressive mankind and save them from themselves. If peoples irrationally in their ignorance rejected this system (they had called it democracy after the Greek city state method of direct representation alongside a slave-underclass) then they had to be taught a lesson, until the survivors submitted to being granted this liberty. The world imposition of democracy of course meant the struggle of the centuries was over. The future was free of conflict, in its place came shopping and limitless sexual practice, meaningful and guiltless. History had come to an end.

Unfortunately – for them – this was a fantasy imposed on the ignorant masses of simple folks. Chateaubriand had explained it in the middle of the Revolution which has lasted since then:

"...ce n'est pas l'homme qui arrête le temps, c'est le temps qui arrête l'homme."

It is not man who stops time, it is time which stops man.

The policy of the imposition of democracy has specific conditions without which it cannot fulfil its purpose, which is, of course, to be a firewall between the financial élite and the impoverished masses. The first condition is the universal franchise. This means a political class and leadership chosen by a vast number of people whose only requirement is that they are registered voters. Uneducated, illiterate, often victims of a most sophisticated 'marketing' by media in turn controlled and owned by the Sect, psychotics among the neurotics, academics among the ignorant – this vast conglomerate selects that figure who, somehow, has managed to please them all. The lowest common denominator.

The second condition is that the elected are appointed to a multi-party governing body which is intended to produce a ruling party versus an opposition. The resulting verbal battlefield is supposed to demonstrate the society's freedom to debate and achieve majority decisions. This model derives from the Assembly of the French Revolution, which at the height of the Terror had the State Prosecutor propose the setting-up of a guillotine between the opposing parties to remind them continually that power lay elsewhere.

The effect of this comical system is a constant switching from government of Party A to government of Party B and so on, each having been appointed through proving the incompetence and corruption of the previous regime.

Thus an election is founded on political promises. Government is founded on a failure to fulfil its promise. A change of government is merely a re-phased set of promises.

The third and dominant condition is that government must not interfere with the market. The market, as has been indicated, represents the coded political term for the financial nexus, the unique domain of the unelected and one-party system that represents a growing and near-total amount of the world's wealth, land and commodities, the Dominio of the Sect.

The leading legalist of the last century, Carl Schmitt, defined sovereign power as being manifest not in the normal running of affairs but rather when the rule of exception is imposed. This implies that when a crisis demanding a suspension of the norm occurs, the special rules reveal the true identity of the power brokers.

Plato, in 'The Republic', stated: "One of the penalties for refusing to participate in politics is that it results in being governed by your inferiors." Since everybody now numbingly admits that we are governed by our inferiors, for the Platonic insight to be acceptable it must be posited that 'politics' lies elsewhere. The instruments, indices, and personnel of power are not to be found inside the democratic module. The imposition of special rules, the suspension of the norms of judicial procedure, the abolition of ancient rights regarding arrest and trial unmask the true nature of democracy – a rhetoric of human rights masking a totalitarian tyranny.

It follows that 'refusing to participate in politics' means refusing to engage in those constructive procedures which will lead to the dismantling of the Revolutionary Caste's institutions, instruments and membership, and refusing to go beyond the doctrine of democracy in order to restore the ancient pre-Revolutionary civic rights and social principles of leadership which had been the spinal column of European civilisation up until the beginning of the Great Interregnum.

Men are inhibited from confronting the Leviathan. Conditioned and prepared not to resist let alone overthrow the system, it is now openly realised that contemporary man experiences himself as helpless. Told that their freedom lies in individuality, they have been convinced that their isolation is the gift of the social order. Do not make waves. Stay in the middle, the extremes destroy. Philip Rieff, a leading Freudian psycho-analyst, openly committed psychoanalysed modern man: "to an active resignation in matters as they are, to a modest hope, and to a satisfiable desire. ... Psychological man ... like his predecessor, the man of the market economy ... understands morality as that which is conducive to increased activity. The important thing is to keep going!" Liberty has been reduced to an active resignation. Equality has been confirmed by a universal granting of credit. Fraternity is assured now we are all debtors. Your debt is personal. Your religion is personal. Your ballot is secret. History, your history too, has come to an end.

Resistance to the Revolution has proved pointless. At the point of challenge a man is outlawed. He is against reason, the peace society demands and deserves, the International Community. His attack is anarchic and merits punishment. It is terror and terrorism is the enemy of the State. The terrorist can not succeed. If he blows up a building – the insurance will collect. If there are victims – a rock concert will raise the money for the families. If the terror increases, the Police will double their brief, their budget and their access to new techniques of torture. Democracy is for ever, and that is that.

The crack in the golden bowl – is the inadequacy, the sheer human inadequacy of the Sect's members. Its leaders are irretrievably lost, weak and insecure. Worse than this, however, is that no matter the one they put forward to defend their bulimic hold on wealth, that person does so without legitimacy. These people have acquired the world's wealth by a deception, by a theft. It is the illegality of their claim, the illegitimacy of their inheritance that shows them up to be usurpers. This means people, by definition, of low and despicable character.

What, therefore, is the path to that new Nomos on the earth, called for by Carl Schmitt, Heidegger, Jünger, and yearned for by the unrepresented millions enslaved by democratic process?

Firstly, the issue of legitimacy must be grasped profoundly, for even civic law has over the last century tried to eliminate it by altered inheritance laws, the reduction of marriage from a legal to an emotional contract, and the transfer of identity from family linkage to credit worthiness. The clarification of this vital matter is, not accidentally, to be found at the very primal and formative stage of that model on which was established the modern structuralist State.

1802 saw the purging of the Tribunat with Napoleon sending four Jacobins to the guillotine accused of a 'conspiracy of daggers', intending his assassination. Urged on by this chastisement, the Tribunat asked that he be given 'a striking sign of national recognition.' The Senate promptly agreed to extend his mandate as First Consul for ten years. He engendered the political discourse along the lines of his desire – continuous power, hereditary principle, with its logical conclusion monarchy. Next, he moved the Council of State to organise a referendum to approve his appointment as Consul for life. On the 2nd August 1802, on a strong turnout, he received 3,653,600 Yes, against 8,272 No. His formidable Chief of Police lost his portfolio for having opposed the referendum. The Constitution was amended to allow him to name his successor. Step by step Napoleon prepared the nation for Empire. Josephine had Maids of Honour appointed to accompany her. Pauline Bonaparte's husband, General Leclerc, on his death was honoured by Court mourning. Murat, husband of Caroline Bonaparte, was appointed Governor of Paris. Napoleon's profile appeared on the new coins. It took the 'Great Conspiracy' of 1804 to grant him his final move to the throne.

From the beginning of 1804 the police had been opening up a major conspiracy led by the great Cadoudal, head of the Chouan movement that formed the Brittany dimension of the Vendée liberation movement. He had brought thousands of men into the struggle, and even after the final defeat of the liberation forces in 1793 he had sustained the Chouan resistance into the Napoleonic era. Without interruption he had gone on fighting the usurpers, firstly the Revolutionaries then the Napoleonic State. Guerilla warfare turned inevitably towards conspiracy. Cadoudal's men planned to capture Napoleon on the road to the

Chateau Malmaison, which with its 260 hectares he had bought for Josephine. At the same moment 'a Prince' was to enter French territory and restore the monarchy.

By utter fabrication Fouché's security system arrived at the conclusion that the intended Prince was the young Duc d'Enghien, grandson of the Grand Condé. The significance of this choice – Condé as key conspirator – must not be lost for it sheds a cold light on Napoleon. Firstly, Le Grand Condé had been the most renowned French General of the Bourbon Dynasty. Secondly, Condé's other reputation was as Frondeur, that is to say, an aristocratic leader of La Fronde, which had sought not to destroy the monarchy but to rescue it from absolutism.

The counter-plot was to arrest Cadoudal and his accomplices in Paris and at the same time to kidnap the Duc d'Enghien. French soldiers were to cross out of France into Baden, take the Prince by force to the Chateau de Vincennes, stage a trial, and then have him summarily shot. On the night of March 21, Enghien, after what was more of a sentencing than a trial, was taken out and shot in the dark by lanternlight in the castle dungeon. In an illegal, clandestine operation, offending both national and international law, the inheritor of the Revolutionary State had assassinated not only the grandson of France's greatest warrior, but also in his person a popular young hero of both the monarchists and the people, for he was also Louis de Bourbon.

Senator Fouché, restored to office by the First Consul, as the expert in clandestine operations, with his dirty work at Vincennes achieved, could complete his task. With a Bourbon Prince murdered the Revolutionary Left could become the instigators of the call to Empire.

March 27, barely a week after the crime, Fouché called the Senate to invite the First Consul to "complete the achievement by making himself as immortal as his glory." Fouché was a typical Empire courtier, the arriviste who had arrived. He had voted for the death of Louis XVI, he presided over Robespierre's downfall, he aided Napoleon's coup d'État on the 18th of Brumaire. Later he would serve as minister for Louis XVIII. The consummate political animal, he could be both accomplice and critic of the dangerous act. His piercing comment on the murder of the Duc d'Enghien found the Heel of Achilles: "It was worse than a crime. It was a mistake!"

As the details leaked out the damage spread. The sordidness of the execution made more intense the moral outrage. They refused to let D'Enghien communicate with Napoleon, a further proof that it had been ordered directly by him. The summary arraignment was made to the sound of his grave being dug. Louis XVIII returned the Order of the Toison d'Or to the King of Spain, since Bonaparte had received the decoration. Gustav-Adolfus, who had begged Napoleon not to execute the Prince, the letter arrived too late, in turn sent back his Cordon of the Aigle-Noir to the King of Prussia for the same reason. These gestures, although belonging to a social order already condemned by the Revolution, nevertheless indicated the first drawing-back from the Napoleonic project, which in time would be activated fatally into a drawing-together of what would become that Alliance destined to finish his Empire at the last.

On 21 March, at Malmaison, Napoleon looked at his watch and announced to Josephine, "The Duc d'Enghien has been shot." On 19 March, France's most renowned writer dressed to attend the gathering at the Tuileries where Napoleon would meet the assembled dignitaries. Chateaubriand had, and would maintain even after the

Emperor's downfall, a dual attitude to Bonaparte. In his sublime masterpiece, 'Memoires d'outre-tombe', he wrote, "...this man, whose genius I admire and whose despotism I despise, this man's tyranny envelops me as in another solitude..."

On that day, his admiration still dominant, and still in Bonaparte's diplomatic service, Chateaubriand went to the reception. The gallery was full. Napoleon was accompanied by Murat and an Aide-de-camp. He moved swiftly among the guests. Chateaubriand noted: "The closer he came to me the more I was struck by the change in his face: his cheeks were fallen and ghostly, his eyes bleary, his appearance pale and troubled, his state dark and dreadful. The attraction which had formerly drawn me to him, stopped; instead of remaining in his path, I made a move to avoid him. He looked at me as if trying to recognise me, took several steps towards me, then turned and moved away. Had I appeared to him like a warning? His Aide had seen me; when the crowd closed in on me the Aide tried to keep sight of me among the people around me and guided the Consul towards me. This game continued for nearly quarter of an hour, with me pulling back and Napoleon following me, well aware. I could not make sense of what had got into the Aide-de-

Camp. Did he take me for someone suspicious he had never seen? Or, knowing who I was, did he want to force Napoleon to meet me? Whatever it was, Napoleon moved into another salon. Satisfied that I had done my duty in appearing at the Tuileries, I left. From the joy I always experience on leaving a castle it is clear that I was not meant to enter them.

"On my return to the Hotel-de-France I said to some of my friends: 'There must be something strange that we don't know about, for Bonaparte could not change as much as this, at least unless he is ill.'"

One of his friends was so struck by this that he wrote, confirming it: "Returning from the First Consul, M. de Chateaubriand declared to his friends that he had observed in the First Consul a great alteration in his appearance and something sinister in his look."

Two days later, between eleven and noon, while walking near the Rue de Rivoli, Chateaubriand heard cried out in the street: "'The judgment of the Special Military Commission meeting at Vincennes has condemned to death Louis-Antoine-Henri de Bourbon, born 2 August, 1772 at Chantilly." He continued: "'This shout hit me like a thunderbolt: it changed my life just as it changed the life of Napoleon. I returned home and I said to Madame de Chateaubriand, 'The Duc d'Enghien has just been shot.' I sat at my desk and wrote my resignation. Madame de Chateaubriand did not oppose me but with great courage stood by me as I wrote. She was well aware of the danger I was in: the trial of [the conspirators] General Moreau and Georges Cadoudal had started: the lion had tasted blood, and this was not the moment to annoy it."

This illustrious death freed Chateaubriand for the great task of his masterpiece and at the same time it cleared the final obstacle on Napoleon's path to crown himself Emperor.

Cadoudal, the last of the great giants of the Liberation War of La Vendée, declared on the scaffold of the guillotine: "We wanted to return a King to France, and we have given France an Emperor!" Much later Chateaubriand reflected that if he had stayed with Bonaparte he, Chateaubriand, would have lost, while Napoleon at St. Helena reflected that if Chateaubriand had stayed with him he, Napoleon, would have won.

The great writer, however, had no doubts: his

life "would have been deprived of what makes character and honour: poverty, struggle, and independence."

Chateaubriand had no doubt, beyond all the certain long-term political consequences of this event, that it was here and at this moment that Bonaparte betrayed his own genius and honour and greatness, and the flaw in Napoleon meant nothing less than the inescapable flaw of the structuralist State. He pours scorn on the Memorial of Las-Cases. He calls Las-Cases, adoring and credulous, with Napoleon "like Hercules suspending men from his mouth by chains of gold." Napoleon wove his fiction of the D'Enghien murder. "I learned afterwards, my dear, that he was favourable to me; they assured me that he spoke not without admiration; and there however – the distributive justice here below!" Chateaubriand does not let this duplicity escape him. "M. le comte de Las-Cases declares that Bonaparte would have pardoned enthusiastically a man who was not guilty!" Relentlessly, he continues, "...he could not make his conscience submit the same way he had made the world submit." In this famous, but today discreetly ignored, paragraph Chateaubriand reaches down to the profoundest spiritual depths of political action.

"Doubtless Bonaparte regarded as the mark of a dominant spirit this sentence which he put down to his compunction as a great man: 'My dear, there, however, the distributive justice here below.' A truly philosophical tenderness! What impartiality! How it justifies by putting to the account of destiny the evil that has come from us! One thinks all excused now that one has called out: 'What do you expect? It was my nature, it was human infirmity.' Someone kills his father, then repeats: 'I am made like that!' And the crowd remain lips sealed, and they examine the skull of this power and they recognise that it was MADE LIKE THAT. And what does it matter to me that you were made like that! Must I submit to your way of being? It would be a fine chaos in the world if all the men who are MADE LIKE THAT, came and wanted to impose themselves one lot on the other. Since one cannot efface their mistakes one makes them divine; one makes a dogma of their wrongs, one turns their sacrileges into religion, and one is considered an apostate should one renounce from the cult of their iniquities."

He concludes that there is a grave lesson to be learned from the life of Bonaparte. "Two actions, two bad actions, began and led to his downfall: the death of the Duc d'Enghien, the war in Spain. ...

He perished on that very side of him which he believed to be strong, profound, invincible, because he violated the moral laws by neglecting and disdaining his true force, that is to say, his superior qualities in order and equity."

Bonaparte's corruption had begun. It was remarkable how outwardly visible it was, confirming the experience of Chateaubriand, as a close examination of his portraits reveal. It is not maturity, nor excess weight, it is this other matter. He appears to be two people, the one before, poetic, inspiring, a leader; the one after, dark, brooding, tyrannical.

The Russian Cabinet vigorously protested the murder, which prompted Bonaparte to reply openly through Le Moniteur, insulting Russia in the process. At St. Petersburg a funeral service was held and on the Cenotaph it read: To the Duc d'Enghien quem devoravit bellua corsica (To the Duc d'Enghien, devoured by the Corsican monster). Chateaubriand notes: "Napoleon believed himself revenged the night he slept in Moscow. Alexander was only satisfied when he entered Paris."

In July 1804, by democratic mandate, a national referendum voted 3,572,329 Yes, against 2,569 No, to the election of Bonaparte as Emperor Napoleon.

Election is not and cannot be legitimation. It is a political instrument, mathematical and manipulable. It is to submit, in every case, to an apparent lottery of chance, what is predetermined in prior organisation.

Legitimacy is an existential and verifiable principle of ownership and power. It is not an accident that the three great dictators of modern times did not even have legitimacy of country, and yet were elected to power by a massive majority.

Napoleon was not French, he was Corsican.
Stalin was not Russian, he was Georgian.
Hitler was not German, he was Austrian.

Legitimacy is an inescapable political reality. Look at how Bonaparte reduced himself to a European laughing-stock in his quest to achieve what he imagined he had extinguished in the Duc d'Enghien. The all-powerful guardian of the Revolution, who had witnessed the regicide of Louis XVI and was friend to Robespierre's brother, plunged into an emotional bid to establish a dynasty. A linked dynasty, secure, legitimised by marriage into an already established dynasty, and of all people, the Hapsburg Dynasty. Marie-Antoinette became Napoleon's aunt, as she lay headless in a Paris grave. What greater proof of the resonance of legitimacy? Yet, it is not absolute, and the dynasties disintegrate, become worthless, disgraceful – the Bourbons proved it.

Yet it must be confirmed that while dynasties collapse and die, by that same active principle they come into being. This is a fundamental element of men in leadership. It is that realistic recognition that the electoral structuralist system, Revolution, or its synonym democracy, tries to eliminate. It is this illusion of the permanence of the State that lies at the core of the Great Interregnum, the perpetual Revolution.

The coming into being of a dynasty represents a usurpation and a new legitimation. The beginning of a dynasty almost certainly results from the accession to power of a figure of renewal, vowed to establish peace after war, or order after anarchy. A hero.

The great founding dynasty of England, the Plantagenets, came into power when Henry II ascended the Throne on 25 October, 1154. A reformer, he was the founder of the English Common Law. He established a sound administration and a justice system.

After him came Richard I, and then came King John. It was in his name that the great legal document, the Magna Carta, was signed. This document, drawn up to deal with contemporary grievances, ended up enshrining important laws protecting the individual from false arrest and imprisonment, and assuring due right to trial. When these rights were removed from the statute books where they had stood, protectively, for almost 900 years, the abrogating laws were passed by a 'democratic' government presided over by an elected Prime Minister who held absolute power, unchecked even by Cabinet, it having become a service instrument of the Leader.

After King John came Henry III, then Edward I, then Edward II, then Edward III, then Richard II. The death of Richard led to the first major trauma of the dynasty. The usurpation was the murder of Richard II, certainly unfit to rule, and the legitimation was that Henry IV, the usurper, was legitimised being the son of John of Gaunt, third son of Edward III. Then came his son, Henry V. After him, his son Henry VI. With Henry VI, weak and at the end half mad, comes the final stage of the great dynasty which was to come crashing down in the 'Wars of the Roses', the conflict between the two great Houses of York and Lancaster. After Henry VI came the 'Yorkist' Edward IV, then, King for a few months, Edward V.

So, the House of Lancaster ruled from Henry IV, V, and VI, all within the wider Plantagenet inheritance. From Edward IV came the return to the House of York, a rule which ended with the reign of Richard III, slandered with genius by Shakespeare. The usurpation was the defeat of Richard III, the legitimation came with Henry VII, his marriage symbolised a union of the warring Houses. Plantagenet rule was over. Tudor rule had begun.

The chronicle of Plantagenet rule was the principal meditation of England's greatest play-wright. In his epic sweep of their dynasty, Shakespeare was able both to narrate and explore the themes of power, of family conflict, of loyalty and treachery. Living as he was at the height of the Tudor epoch he had traced back a historical gratitude to Henry Tudor. Henry is the liberating usurper ushering in England's greatest epoch. For if his son, Henry VIII, was the greatest of all

England's monarchs, who had dragged England out of the medieval age and freed his people from enslavement to the ignorance and superstition of Pope and Rome, he was also the dynastic ruler who left his country his daughter, Elizabeth. It was during her years of peace that England's culture reached its highest point, giving the world Shakespeare, Marlowe and the Elizabethan theatre, but Elizabeth could not rule. She was the prototype of the symbolic ruler of democracy in the future, powerless, the signature at the foot of the document. She ruled a State governed by the aristocratic class that Henry had forged over decades. They were to rule England up to the middle of the 20th century.

The tragic anarchy of the Wars of the Roses marks the end of the dynasty that signals the end of an epoch. Henry Tudor marks a new beginning, a new dynasty founded on reason after unreason. Henry VII was the natural, if illegal, heir to the Lancastrian claim to the Throne. His decision to marry Elizabeth of York allowed him to go before the nation as the unifier of the red and white roses of Lancaster and York. The 118 years of Tudor rule mark the summit of the English State. Because Tudor's claim to legitimacy was slender he found himself obliged to lean heavily on the symbolic and semiotic instruments of power. As a result he rescued the medieval signs of legitimacy and inheritance from the defunct medieval world that had destroyed itself in chivalric conflicts. He elevated them as a semiotics which signalled a Tudor rule over a united State. Chivalry became courtesy and a new and refined Kingly court emerged. Henry's son was educated in the manners and style of chivalry, but what had decimated the great baron houses of the past now had become a civic form of blending and connecting the great families. It was at the youthful tournaments and jousting that Henry VIII learned the statecraft and even the musicianship that were to be his style. Erasmus was his teacher and soon Henry was ready for his life's task, to bring England into the modern world. His father in his need for legitimacy had reached beyond the Plantagenets, linking his House with the Normans, the Saxons, back to the legendary British King Arthur and the Welsh Prince Cadwaladr whose red dragon flew on his standard.

Henry VIII represents the summit of Kingship. What follows, therefore, represents the senescence of the State. Elizabeth is Queen in name and signature but already the aristocracy, set up by Henry to web the nation in a set of landed gentry families which could hold the country together by a mutual self-interested loyalty, had taken power.

A dépassement of the Napoleonic disaster has to be made. It was illegitimacy seizing power and 'crowning' itself, leading directly to downfall, since the State had been rigidly designed along structuralist methods, leaving in its wake the headless State, systematic, functioning, yet doomed to a much greater failure than that of the man, Napoleon. In the end the Jacobins had won. Napoleon's usurpation had been double, that of Kingship and that of Revolution. When his head fell (a political guillotining) the body remained, the modern atheist State founded on his and the American lawyers' Code. As the Revolution's executioner could have explained – after the head is cut it goes on talking for a time, and the body twitches false signs of life even to the grave. Since it is now time to bury the body of Democracy, it is also time to tap into those constants that have always governed human behaviour in all recorded history, and abandon the frivolous musings of Diderot and Rousseau.

It is time to return to a visible leadership and an open loyalty.

VI

At this point it can be recognised that with the French Revolution a new social system came into being. Its implications were far-reaching. It was not a French phenomenon but rather took on an apocalyptic and world significance. In the process it abolished monarchy, and with it consigned the concept of monarchy to the dustbin of history. Monarchy was declared an anachronism. It was not modern. At the trial of Louis XVI the Montagnards declared: "Louis Capet is guilty of having been King." In the process the Revolution abolished religion, the word religion being from the Latin, religio, to bind together. The modern, that is Revolutionary State was atheist by its inner necessity. The State was the binding factor. When Napoleon permitted the Catholic Church to return it was to be as a reductive system, devoid of Papal, that is decisive ruling power, education and even obligations.

"Your rites are dead, your creeds are dead
Your social order too,
Where tarries here the man who said
'See! I make all things new.'"

Religion was redefined as 'belief' and in turn consigned to the dustbin of the Unconscious.

What came in place of the natural social cycles of personal rule was the 'headless' structuralist State. Its primary élite were the political class, the Legislators. Representatives and Presidents came and went, behind them, the institutions of police and army remained, unchanging and unelected. Yet over that time, from the Assignats, the paper credit-note money of the Revolution, the banking class, slowly, step by step emerged from the evolutionary swamps of 'modernity', finally to dominate the landscape, carnivorous monsters ready to devour the herbivorous talking-class of the Legislators. The Sect had taken over the forest.

It has been the take-over of the Sect, warned against by so many great writers and thinkers, which went un-noticed and misunderstood by the masses. It is that power system which, having reached its apogee at the turn of the 20th century, now is in process of irreversible decline and collapse.

The end of the monarchic epoch can be dated over two stages and in two places, although the end of that epoch has other dates and places of political consequence and significance.

The Great Interregnum began in 1793 with the guillotining of Louis XVI and Marie-Antoinette. With the end of monarchy came the end of womanhood. Marie-Antoinette was not executed as Queen of France, but as a woman. The abolition of monarchy was the abolition of inheritance. The abolition of inheritance was the abolition of the family. The end of the family was the beginning of humanism. The beginning of humanism was the abolition of womanism. Woman had been abolished. Under the Terror the 'humans' shaved the heads of women collaborators with the Ancien Régime. In the Liberation of 1944 the 'humans' shaved the heads of thousands of women collaborators with the German occupation.

The other key date opening the Great Interregnum was 1909, when the forces of the uprising of the city of Istanbul, led by the Rebel, Mustafa Riza, later named Ataturk, in defiance of his own oath of allegiance, stormed the Palace and dethroned Sultan Abdulhamid Khan II, to the cries of 'Liberté, Fraternité, Egalité.' The Sultanate itself was not formally abolished until 1922.

Now the end of the Great Interregnum has arrived. It is appropriate that its imminent disappearance be examined, to recognise that in-back process which will activate its inevitable demise. In order to view this full eclipse the eyes must be able to observe closely and avoid being blinded by the dazzling event. To facilitate the investigation it is necessary to choose a guide who is neither a product of the decline under examination, nor a prey to the outdated dialectics of the present system, or even its media simplifications.

The approaches to the event will therefore be through an ancient master and a modern one. Ibn Khaldun (born Tunis 1332) and Ernst Jünger (born Heidelberg 1895).

To a generation fed on movies and television there is no direct access to the world-view of preceding generations, let alone the preceding centuries. Part of the abolition of history has been its reconstruction for the masses as entertainment, the sub-text always being that that was 'then' and this is 'now', are we not lucky to have missed the bad old days!

The collapse of the Sect's social order was well understood by the great writers of the 19th century at the very moment the Sect could point to its greatest hegemonic triumph.

Wagner's incomparable and gigantic music-drama, 'The Ring of the Nibelung' was, even at the time, recognised as announcing the end of an age. Its significance lay in his profound insight that the power of the élite, the Gods, lay not in their position but in their possessions. The Gods take absolute power by entering their castle, Valhalla. Their rule is sustained no longer by their warrior-class, the Valkyrie, but by owning the Ring. The Ring, made from the gold of the Nibelung, permits them to wield absolute power. The gold itself is no longer needed. Throughout the drama it remains guarded in a cave until Siegfried slays Fafner, the dragon who protects it. The gold in the cave, real capital, is never used. The Ring, the magical dimension of gold, is enough to give power. The function of power is increase. Increase in the transaction is usury itself.

The core of the epic is the emergence of the hero whose necessary condition is that he should have no fear. Thus he is able to kill Fafner and pass through the ring of fire to release the Valkyrie, Brunnhilde, with a kiss. It is by the awakening of woman, who it will be remembered had been abolished to open the way to 'humanism' and the bankers' misogynist Sect, that the new era is announced. It is the warrior woman who avenges the male hero victim, Siegfried, and returns the Ring to its natural place in nature, the river. The Rhine, receiving the Ring, and thus the gold, overflows its banks, inundating the domain of the Gods, Valhalla.

The end of a whole social order, its gods, its heroes, its evaluations – everything is swept away. The amazing, cathartic finale to the epic comes with the vast relief that it is all over, the Age is finished. Yet it is a vision of hope, for while Brunnhilde in her immolation leaps in an oblivion to re-unite with her lover, so the people, the masses, turn to face a new beginning, a new order, what Carl Schmitt designated as a new Nomos on the earth.

The other great giant of the 19th century was Henrik Ibsen, the Norwegian playwright. Through his life's works he plunged deeper and deeper into the depths of the century's engulfing nihilism.

In 'Ghosts' the youth infected by syphilis sinks into madness and darkness asking for the sun. In 'The Wild Duck' the young girl commits suicide when the ugly truth of the adult world destroys her. In 'The Masterbuilder' the great architect flings himself to his death from the top of his great tower. In his verse-play, 'Brand', his hero is submerged in an avalanche. In 'Hedda Gabler' his heroine shoots herself. In 'Rosmersholm' the couple Rosmer and Irene walk into the mill-race to drown. In 'John Gabriel Borkman' his bankrupted hero dies on the mountain on the ice-cold summit. In his last masterpiece, 'When We Dead Awaken', his couple, Rubek and Irene, are engulfed in an avalanche.

Rilke called his work "A Last Judgment. A Finality." In 'The Notebooks of Malte Laurids Brigge' he made his famous tribute to Ibsen and his work.

"...What did you care if a woman stayed or left, if this man was seized by vertigo and that one by madness, if the dead were alive and the living seemed dead: what did you care? It was all so natural for you; you passed through it the way someone might walk through a hall and didn't stop. But you lingered, bent over, where our life boils and precipitates and changes colour: inside. Farther in than anyone has ever been; a door had sprung open before you, and now you were among the alembics in the firelight. In there, where, mistrustful, you wouldn't take anyone with you, in there you sat and discerned transitions. And there, since your blood drove you not to form or to break, but to reveal, there you made the enormous decision so to magnify these tiny events, which you yourself first perceived only in test tubes, that they would be seen by thousands of people, immense before them all. Your theatre came into being. ... You were there, and everything that is barely measurable – an emotion that rises by half a degree, the angle of reflection, read off from up close, of a will burdened by an almost infinitesimal weight, the slight cloudiness in a drop of longing, and that barely perceptible colour-change in an atom of confidence – all this you had to determine and record. For it is in such reactions that life existed, *our* life, which had slipped into us so deeply that it was hardly possible even to make conjectures about it any more.

"Because you were a revealer, a timelessly tragic poet, you had to transform this capillary action all at once into the most convincing gestures, into the most available forms. So you began that unprecedented act of violence in your work, which, more and more impatiently, desperately, sought equivalents in the visible world for what you had seen inside. There was a rabbit there, an attic, a room where someone was pacing back and forth; there was a clatter of glass in a nearby bedroom, a fire outside the windows; there was the sun. There was a church, and a rock-strewn valley that was like a church. But this wasn't enough: finally towers had to come in and whole mountain ranges; and the avalanches that bury landscapes spilled onto a stage overwhelmed with what is tangible, for the sake of what cannot be grasped."

The dramatic worlds of the two great masters are essentially the one envisioned reality of the usury-based bourgeoisie. In both sets of dramas there is a quite new vision, that of man seeking escape or rather liberation from the doomed society. The Masterbuilder's Tower and Valhalla, the sea and the avalanche mirror the Rhine and the engulfing flames of Götterdämmerung. The man's liberation in both epics is dependent on the rescuing woman. The drama of 'Hedda Gabler' is not her suicide, but its cause – her failure to win over her lover to a mutual immolation. In all the other Ibsen tragedies it is the sacrificial couple who accomplish a spiritual illumination in their end, as Brunnhilde's leap into the flames is her union with Siegfried. The destruction of a whole world is accomplished by the liberating couple.

The bourgeois ethos of the Sect was based on a doctrinal misogynism that is the core reality of the Republic whose fathers are Robespierre and Saint-Just, the celibate high priests of democracy who had confirmed their ruthless philosophy not just with the immolation of monarchy, killing Louis XVI as King but Marie-Antoinette as woman, and, as if to leave no doubt, the execution of their own friends, Camille Desmoulins and his wife. There could be no Revolutionary Couple.

From this, the highest spiritual and intellectual twin summit of the bourgeois age, the works of Wagner and Ibsen, there may therefore be extrapolated the first necessary principle of the new Nomos of the coming age. At its core must be found a couple, that liberating couple which finds the woman upholding her beloved spouse's project for mankind and womankind.

The death-throes of the bourgeois epoch thus represent, prior to this emergence, the final writhing agony of the despairing male ferocity whose political face is terrorism. Terrorism is not and cannot be perceived as the destructive force of an evil 'other'. It is not even a Janus-head of one monster. It is the quintessential core of the dying entity. Dostoevsky's 'Demons' is the clinical analysis of terror, the uniquely modern form of a society's suicide. Terror is born out of the belly of the beast it has emerged to destroy. It has a set of discrete entities, all of which are specific elements already in the society, which only demand that they are aligned together like a series on a Rubik's Cube, at that point, there is the act itself. Terrorism's necessary elements are – a tyrannical and unjust regime, a dissatisfied under-class, a secret security police, police infiltration, media mis-information, a prior corruptible intellectual class of liberals, and gullible discontented and dispossessed men. In its first stage, host society and its terrorists are one. In its second stage, it turns on the society, that is, on itself. In the third stage, the terrorists are crushed and the people oppressed by security laws. In the fourth stage, the State is obliged actively to set up terrorist events, thus returning to the first stage. It is at that point that the State is structurally doomed. The terrorists did not do it, since they are no more. The State has committed suicide. The last words of Dostoevsky's 'Demons' follow the discovery of the nihilist Stavrogin's suicide.

"Everything indicated pre-meditation and consciousness to the last minute. Our medical men, after the autopsy, completely and emphatic-ally ruled out insanity."

Nihilism, suicide and terrorism are synonyms. They are not a political doctrine, rather, they are the failure of politics. It is an end-game, yet it cannot be said that after it comes nothing. It IS the 'nothing'. After it comes a new beginning. A new Nomos.

In 'The Muqaddima' Ibn Khaldun outlined the three stages through which man, as a collective animal, passes. In this dynamic model there is no concept of stasis. It is, therefore, a completely other view of human society from that brought into being by the French Revolution, that of the atheist and rationalist politicians of the self-styled Enlightenment which has plunged the world into darkness. Ibn Khaldun considered that the primal stage of men as society begins with what he defined as Bedouinism. This First Stage of itself implies a dynamic movement of men in contra-distinction to a prior settled culture.

Bedouinism is not, he insists, nomadism. Nomadism implies a settled and organic community identified by its capacity and habit of movement from a place to a place for pasture or market.

The Bedou is outside the urban system. The Bedou is cut off from the urban entity even if he is in it. In modern times, by application of his model this permits of the term being applied to Districtism or Townshipism.

At a certain stage the Bedouin in their power of growth and expansion, and by a genetic vitalisation denied the passive urban community, begin to identify themselves as a new civic force. A natural need becomes wedded to a higher evaluation, an evaluation of themselves. There emerges among them the most powerful force that social man can experience. It is kinship, but not of blood. It transcends the tribal and the familial. This unification of the group takes them to the Second Stage. Stage Two is defined by Ibn Khaldun with the term 'Asabiyya'. Asabiyya, normally 'kinship', is here used to mark as distinctive the bond, the life and death unifying bond of a brotherhood without blood ties. In the excellent Pléiade edition of 'The Muqaddima' its editor and translator calls it 'esprit de corps', but it is much more than that, for it has in it also a moral evaluation as in the term 'Futuwwa', chivalry or nobility of character. Asabiyya unites men to find the power to act and transform and command. If its motor power is high, its brotherhood is raised higher. If the binding factor (religio – to bind together) is there, that is Divine religion, it is, that being its highest possibility, assured a triumph.

The Pinçon critique observed a unifying element that linked the Sect's priesthood of wealth. However, the mathematical model on which they have acquired their wealth is pre-determined continually to impoverish others, which means that as the wealth increases, the wealthy themselves decrease in number. This mutually assured destruction is the evidentiary failure of their social posture of unity as a class. Each is an enemy. It is the inability of the Sect to bond together, that is to say, their negation of genuine Asabiyya, that unmasks the fact of their having passed below it.

That group – the new Bedouin – are ready to take their impulse to unity to its highest point.

Without Asabiyya the Bedouin remain isolated individuals. The slave is alone. His religion, he has been programmed to accept, is his own private privilege – nobody else's business. This guarantees that they will not pose a threat, except as isolated individuals, that is, criminals.

The Bedouin who cannot engender Asabiyya among themselves are assured continual slavery. Any impulse to unify is taught to be socially disruptive. The only group activities permitted are groups of common interest in sexual practices, sport and concerts. There are social workers to sedate the lowest class and psycho-therapists to assuage the angst of the technical élite. Atheism offers anxiety as its existential fee that must be paid for 'maturity'.

Once belief in the Divine surges through the Bedouin as a group, the Asabiyya takes on its transformative power. At that stage the Asabiyya group recognise that to overcome the isolation principle of the dominant group it is vital that unity is enhanced, indeed guaranteed. The only means to the highest unity is by the appointment of a King. They then pass to Stage Three.

Stage Three is Kingship. The reality of

Kingship is the giving of the oath of allegiance. The appointment of the King transfers that authority to each of the people of Asabiyya. While Scotland was free and strong in culture and identity its leader was 'The King of Scots' – never the King of Scotland. With the King 'over the water' the tyrants could empty the Highlands and replace the shattered Asabiyya of the clans with sheep. Clan Asabiyya is Asabiyya's lowest form, kinship, and so, easily vanquished. The true Asabiyya as understood by Ibn Khaldun is of a higher spiritual brotherhood, which is always, in its great phase, invincible.

It requires a young intellect to grasp Ibn Khaldun – not his ideas but his mode of thinking. The victory of the 'Allies' – of course, deadly enemies – in 1945, imposed dialectical method on philosophy and therefore political discourse. By mid-century only a quartet of intellectuals stood apart from the mass ethos, insisting not just that a whole social system was, in Malaparte's final diagnosis, 'Kaputt', but that the time was moving towards an utterly renewed world order.

Heisenberg was their scientist, whose important contribution was to insist thinking be in terms of a dynamic world of fusion and fission as understood in nuclear physics. The Newtonian model was of a world where the laws of gravity affirmed the billiard-ball solidity of the atom. In the coming ethos the cosmos had to be understood as a realm of whirling matter which if viewed one way was particles and if viewed another way was waves. The Kantian world of categorical imperative and fixed terms bounded by logical processes had given way to paradox, and precision had yielded to models of 'fuzzy' mathematics. The new order could not be a retro-impulse going back to the past. It had to be grounded in the present.

Heidegger was the philosopher of the four. On the occasion of Ernst Jünger being installed as Doctor Honoris Causa at Bilbao University, the present author spoke of Heidegger's importance, and his masterwork, 'Sein und Zeit' (1927):

"This work had changed forever the terms of the philosophical discourse. Heidegger's insight into the nature of technique was the result of his phenomenological exploration of the 'everyday' procedure which resulted from its all-embracing exigencies. This exploration laid bare, or peeled away, those inter-connected relationships of human action, that had hitherto been unquestioned because not isolated and identified, out of the way of assumed factors and unrealised dependencies. Heidegger extricated the human creature in an event of such distinctive character he felt obliged to rename man 'Dasein.' What he had done was nothing less than cast aside the image of man as the enslaved end-product of unconfronted functionality and passivity. He replaced it with a view of man as a project-oriented being, active and engaged in encountering his meanings and his mortality.

"So what Heidegger opened up for the future was nothing less than the phenomenology of freedom, which by implication, laid bare the mechanisms of slavery which made peace look like war, made legislated liberty produce slave camps, abstract research produce nuclear weaponry, and psychotherapy produce passive consumers."

Jünger was the visionary of the quartet. He could be seen as the synthesiser of the world-view that they shared in common. His text, 'Der Arbeiter', made the dépassement of the marxist categories which had heralded that disastrous foray of philosophy down into politics. To Jünger the worker was not the individual proletarian working for his bourgeois owner of the means of production. The worker was each of us as dependent on, submitted to, and participant in, the process of technique.

He wrote: "It remains to destroy the legend according to which the essential quality of the worker is an economic quality."

Moving the discourse out of the marxist realm of political dialectics he framed his thinking in mythic terms.

Speaking of Jünger in the same text quoted above at his installation in Bilbao, the present author explained:

"Jünger gave to this mythic form the name of 'Gestalt.' 'The worker', thus, was not a structural concept, certainly not defined by his structural position within the capitalist frame. Nor did it imply a coherent historical group of labourers.

"What was the Gestalt? Heidegger, in his famous reply to Jünger's text 'Über die Linie' said: 'For you, Jünger, the Gestalt stands for what is only accessible in a seeing, to be found in this seeing, which among the Greeks was called 'Idein' – a word which Plato employed for a look which considered not the changing of sense perception, but the immutable, the being, the 'idea'. You also characterise the Gestalt as the Calm Being. The Gestalt is certainly not an 'idea', in the sense of the meaning of modern philosophy, any more than it is by consequence a regulative representation in the sense of Kant.'

"Heidegger preferred to locate the Gestalt of Jünger as a Nietzschean event. Heidegger hailed the work as a weighty achievement, having done what no prior Nietzschean work had done. He said, 'It had undertaken to make possible an experience of being and of the way in which it is, in the light of the Nietzschean project of being and "will to power".'

"Despite this impressive Heideggerian definition, one must take into account Jünger's own view. In conversation with me, he categorically refuted the idea that the Gestalt was Platonic. He pointed out, 'You cannot SEE a Platonic idea.' Rather, he referred the matter to the great discussion which took place between Schiller and Goethe. There, Goethe made exactly this point, when Schiller defined the Goethean description of the metamorphosis of plants as being merely the Platonic idea. Goethe's concern went much deeper – he was trying to move the modern imagination into a new way of seeing biological phenomena as entities moving through time and thus taking their meaning from their full realisation in nature, from seed to decay."

And further on in the same discourse:

"Jünger identifies modern man as under the Gestalt of the Worker. Each one of them is defined within the all-embracing system of technique. It is in this sense that Heidegger declared Jünger to have defined nihilism for our time. Yet the author's intention was not merely descriptive but pre-scriptive. His viewpoint is that firstly one should accept the vast force-wave engulfing the time, and then prepare the strategy of survival, escape and, ultimately, victory over it. Firstly he announced, 'Bourgeois society is condemned to death.' Then he warned, 'Society is renewed by simulating attacks against itself. Its imprecise character, or rather, its absence of character, permits it to absorb even the most violent negation of itself.'"

The fourth, Carl Schmitt, represents the legalist in the group. It must be understood that there is no equivalent to this formidable quartet of intellectuals. It is the synergistic impact of these four giants that marks them as being the unique guards at the abandoned gateway to the future, negating emphatically the conviction of the Sect that they had cancelled the future to replace it with an eternal non-historical presence that had replaced discourse with consumption. A legalist, a philosopher, a writer and a scientist faced them and agreed that the old order was over. It was time to make life return to the species and the exhausted planet.

The key situation defined in this text is that the political agreement has been transformed into the fiduciary contract. It was Schmitt who first pointed out that the State no longer exists. In 1963 he wrote:

"The State, the model of political unity, which embodied the monopoly of political decision, the State, this work of art, made in a European mould and with Western rationalism, is dethroned."

He pointed out that the two terms 'politics' and 'police' both derive from the Greek word 'polis' – people. The politics had gone – the police remained.

The form of the State is put in question the more its power increases. Schmitt, identifying the sickness of the time, saw that the absolute power arrived at the point that 'the enemy' was abolished. What did this mean? In historical terms – as opposed to modern post-history – the enemy was the other. Two parties face to face. The conflict once resolved, they could continue existence.

Schmitt noted: "The enemy, he also, has his status. He is not a criminal. The limits of war can be imposed on him. ... A normal peace. ... clauses of amnesty. This makes possible a clear distinction between war and peace, and also an unequivocal neutrality."

The new power system refused to recognise the enemy as a human being. He was, in Schmitt's terms, 'hors la loi' and 'hors l'humanité', thus 'pushing war to the extreme limits of the inhumane.'

The initiation of this absolutism has been here identified as finding its prototype in the war of the Vendée which took its character from the Revolutionary government defining the Vendéen population as non-human. This was to be the doctrine that licensed the genocide of the American native nations, the jewish race in Germany, the bourgeois class in Soviet Russia and the resistant Afghan youth in the present time. Once people worldwide, as has now happened, allow themselves to be defined as 'the International Community' — a designation that has been ratified by absolutely no known franchise – at that moment what Schmitt names as 'a total depoliticisation' has taken place and the State has been renounced.

These analyses of Schmitt were written in 1932 ('Der Begriff des Politischen'), 74 years before the revelation of Abu Ghraib in Baghdad being used by the US Army as a centre for the torture and sexual degradation of Iraqi prisoners who had been charged with no crime: before the sequestration of hundreds of Arabs and Afghans in Guantanamo Prison on Cuba where men have been systematically tortured and imprisoned for years with a declared intention *not* to try them: before various nations had participated in the secret and anonymous flight of prisoners by the USA, via Europe, specifically to countries which can torture with impunity. This last barbarism has been openly admitted and given a name: rendition. The Oxford Dictionary defines rendition as "the surrender of a place, garrison, or possession." Men have become possessions. Men have become things. The humanism itself, underlying poetique of the Revolution, has collapsed. The nihilism is complete.

Given the unanimous diagnosis of the four thinkers, Heisenberg, Heidegger, Jünger and Schmitt the meaning, necessity and relevance of the Khaldunian analysis becomes clear. In 'The Muqaddima' Ibn Khaldun defines the matter:

"Asabiyya gives protection, defence and attack, and every enterprise required by belonging to the group.

Men, by their nature, need in every social organisation an authority and arbiter to avoid mutual aggression.

This person must dominate the group, depending on this, on Asabiyya, otherwise he cannot fulfil his task.

That domination is power.

It is more than the simple command.

Indeed, with the command one is simply an obeyed ruler, but one not yet enabled to impose his orders by constraint.

Now, power is the act of domination, and governing by compulsion. When a man, belonging to a powerful group, is in the position of an obeyed leader, he will not fail to exercise domination and constraint if he has the means to do so, for it is something that the soul desires. But he can only succeed thanks to the Asabiyya which grants him permission to be obeyed.

Domination by the exercise of power is thus the ultimate end of Asabiyya. It is thus evident that power is the end of Asabiyya.

When Asabiyya has attained its end, the group has attained power."

It must be re-emphasised that Ibn Khaldun's thinking projects a cyclical view of history that envisages human society curving in a pattern that moves with an evolutionary energy to a point of apogee and then fades down into a decay as in the cycle of seasons and of the human body. It is not a linear fantasy that envisages a utopian end with a society in a stasis of achieved goals. What is incumbent on thinking men is to recognise at what stage of the process they find themselves, and thus activate it and accomplish it, taking into account the different risks and dangers that their point in time imposes on them.

The Third Stage, as mentioned earlier, is Kingship. In detail, this stage in turn has three phases: tyranny, luxury and docility. The first phase should be considered as the high-point of society. In it the Kingship is at its most powerful and beneficial to the people. It is tyranny in the ancient mode of tyrannos as empowered King.

Belloc gives the clearest modern definition of Kingship, that is, monarchy.

"The normal history of mankind furnishes you with Monarchy everywhere. It is only our exceptional time of transition which lacks the institution for the moment.

"I do not mean by the word 'Monarch' a man or woman living in a large house, nor do I mean a man or woman dressed up in a particular fashion. I most certainly do not mean a man who is put up as a revered symbol, or as a machine for signing documents, and denied all real power. I mean any man or woman or child, but normally an adult man, in possession of his faculties, who is responsible ultimately to the commonwealth for the general conduct and preservation of the commonwealth at any moment.

"The definition of Monarchy is that there is one real and attainable human head ultimately responsible in any moment for the fate of society. The leading function of the Monarch is to protect the weak man against the strong, and therefore to prevent the accumulation of wealth in a few hands, the corruption of the Courts of Justice and of the sources of public opinion.

"I say, imagine any (one of these Kings) not through their character, but through the powers granted them by the constitutions of their times, placed at the head of the modern State. What do you think would happen to the corrupt judges, to the politicians who take bribes, to the great trusts that destroy a man's livelihood, to the secret financiers boasting that they control the State? Their blood would turn to water.

"In the great mass of executable acts Monarchy works properly in a society of great numbers because it is *responsible*. An Oligarchy that is not aristocratic – a Parliament, for instance – is never really responsible. You cannot grasp it. You cannot attack it. You can hardly define it. Each individual in such an amorphous executive does harm with impunity because he can always say that it was not he that did it, but some other or some group of others. He and the judicial system form also necessarily all one clique. No parliamentarian, since aristocracy failed in England, has gone to prison for a bribe taken or given. Finally, there is the most cogent argument for Monarchy, contained in my original definition: the force of things."

Ibn Khaldun marks the point at which Asabiyya installs Monarchy as being that point when the King adopts a natural currency based on gold and silver. In the cycle of time the great masterful epoch passes. Ibn Khaldun explains:

"When a group, thanks to its Asabiyya, achieves a certain degree of domination it partakes in a quantity of wealth in proportion to its power and enjoys in its turn prosperity and wellbeing.

"If the group is so powerful that no-one dreams of taking power from them, or sharing it with them, they become satisfied with their wealth and fiscal revenues.

"Their one ambition is to profit from their prosperity, acquire wealth, lead a life of abundance, enjoy tranquillity and ease under the protection of the State, and to adopt the habits of the élite in the matter of housing and clothes, with more and more extravagance and refinement as they get richer and used to luxury and all that follows from it."

Since this is clearly that moment when a new Asabiyya must inevitably arise in response to that identified nihilism which is the immediate present, it is necessary to add to the Khaldunian viewpoint of historical process the Jüngerian vision of the identity of the man of Asabiyya, the one who with his brothers will unite to establish a new Nomos on the earth.

Jünger gives to this new man, and these new men a name. 'Der Waldgang' was written in 1951. Its central Gestalt, using his mythic system of imaging – is the Waldgänger, the one who goes into the forest. He explains:

"It is not a romantic or literal image. ... The Waldgänger is the actual individual, he acts in the specific case. He does not need theories, nor laws cooked up by party legalists, in order to know what is right. ... Here, things become simple if any purity remains in him. We have seen that the great experience of the Forest is the meeting with oneself, the inalterable core of the self, the essence which supports the temporal and individual appearance."

This means that the new man has recognised himself as an in-time creature somehow with a beyond-time contract. However, he does not suggest such a man is an anchorite, cut off from society. He, with them is already surrounded by the bourgeois family, the friends and acquaintances from before the emergence. From his emergence, "There is born a Resistance."

The Resistance is precisely the beginning of the social event Ibn Khaldun identifies as the Asabiyya of the Bedouin.

Jünger makes it plain:

"If in a town of 10,000, we will be content to assume that there are 100 of them who have resolved not to submit to brute force. If in a city of one million there are 10,000 Waldgänger – this is an immense power. It is enough to bring about the fall of the most powerful tyrants."

In the present nihilist epoch Jünger notes that the police are the civic army set to guard the people. Under the doctrine of Security they are obliged to suspect everyone. This splits the State in two, the accused and the accusers. A process that has been a long time evolving has now completely encircled man until his situation is intolerable. It is at this point that the people of spiritual core, and dynamised by it – step forward.

"For we are not just involved in our national disaster, we are caught up in a world catastrophe, in which one is scarcely able to say, let alone prophesy, who are the real winners and who are the losers."

Jünger indicates both the kind of person the Waldgänger is and also what is needed to unify him with like men of heart.

The first indication of such a man is one "who

still knows the difference between gold and printer's ink (on currency)."

He is not an anarchist opposing a mechanical world.

He has turned to the absolute as his source of happiness.

He is not a soldier. He does not know the forms of the military or their discipline. He does not fight by the rules of war yet he is not a gangster. "Once a *people*, a whole people take on this charge, they become an irresistible power."

The Waldgänger, or Bedouin of Asabiyya, has an interiority which is what assures the triumph of the group.

The heart of the matter, as we saw above, is:

"...in der Begegnung mit dem eigenen Ich, dem unverletzbaren Kerne, dem Wesen, aus dem sich die zeitliche und individuelle Erscheinung speist."
"...the meeting with oneself, the inalterable core of the self, the essence which supports the temporal and individual appearance."

Such a man believes "that every man is immortal and eternal life is his," according to Jünger.

Such a man is a Sufi and his religion is Islam, according to Ibn Khaldun.

The works of Jünger and Ibn Khaldun would not be the tremendous texts we can recognise them as being if they were not relevant and applicable to this endgame of nihilism in which, up until now, we have been living.

In fact the Khaldunian/Jüngerian view is directly indicated on three continents: the USA, Europe, and Africa.

In the USA at the Khaldunian stage of Bedouinism can be found three (at present) separate groups.

Firstly, the Mexican population in the USA. They are strictly segregated on the edge of cities, Districtism in action.

Secondly, the American native tribes. They are separate in reservations.

Thirdly, the former black slave population. They too live mainly in special districts or quarters of the great cities and in the country also in the Southern States. However, Islam has begun to spread among their people.

Of these three groups, the Mexicans are only united by family allegiances and by gangs, but they do not as yet indicate men reaching to the higher moral condition that is the prerequisite of Asabiyya. The Amerindians have been profoundly corrupted by the State, which has an excessive fear (guilt) when it comes to the Navaho and the Hopi, a corruption instituted to pre-empt rebellion. They have been granted special concessional rights to run Casinos on the Reservations exempted from the limitation of national law.

The black Americans are the significant and spiritually dangerous grouping. Utterly betrayed and abandoned since the Civil War, even the mid-twentieth century civil rights movement failed to change anything. The 2005 destruction by hurricane in Mississippi once and for all showed that the State has considered its black population as 'other' than its citizenry. Currently, the USA has a prison population statistically akin to the size of the population of Israel. The majority of penitentiary prisoners are black. Islam is now the dominant religious grouping in the USA after Evangelism. It is almost entirely made up from the black population.

In Europe the situation is much more fully evolved and the imminence of Asabiyya emerging is much clearer.

The Bedouin groupings are to be found in every country of the Union, but the most evolved and the ones possessing the beginning of a sense of unity are those in England, France and Germany. Furthermore those Bedouin, an enormous Muslim population, have also three powerful languages, all unified by a common calligraphy. Urdu in England, Arabic in France and (Osmanli, by theoretical extension) Turkish in Germany.

In Africa, emerging after a decade, is a most significant phenomenon of Khaldunian Bedouin-ism. Two of the 'extra' categories of the Apartheid system were imposed on the South African people by the regime, under the guidance of the hindu Ghandi, who recommended a several layer caste system similar to hindu India's. In it, between black and white, came 'coloured', that is those resulting from racial intermarriage, and Indian. In order to further divide and oppress, the regime split the 'coloured' Muslims from the christians by inventing a near-fictional category of 'Cape-Malay'. This, however, resulted in a powerful cementing of the Muslim community. It strengthened its culture, and in the end proved to be the most active and intellectual force of resistance to Apartheid. White rule transferred to black rule, which jealously guarded its new power and revealed itself reluctant to accept the undefinable 'coloureds' since the political pretence was that all were 'citizens' now.

The truth is that inter-racial marriages not only 'breed down' but they also, by strengthening the gene pattern, 'breed up'! Thus a new society has been born, not tied to genealogy or nationalism, but powerfully bonded to a religious story of struggle and survival. Here is a fully ready and powerfully prepared community, marginalised in townships built by a white regime and sustained and accepted by a dominantly black regime. On the margins. United. Powerful in their Islam. Asabiyya has already begun. Such an Asabiyya, given its make-up, will irrevocably sweep into its orbit the new black and white Muslim population, since only their Nomos can offer a life-view that is by definition, colour-blind.

Given the persecution of the European

Muslims, a crude and brutal oppression on a well-educated Muslim populace, it is the State which must be seen – just as much as in South Africa – as being the activating agency of Asabiyya.

This will be the third irradiation of Europe by a settled force inside its established borders. The first was the so-called Barbarian invasion which ended and absorbed the Roman Empire. It was a slow process. It began in battles and settled into trading and local governments. At one stage there was Roman Law. Then at a second stage came the imposition and acceptance of barbarian custom and evaluation. At a third stage a new Europe was born. Day by day the shaven Roman grew his Medieval beard.

The second was the dynamic Viking power that swept over Britain, Northern France and down the Volga to Russia. It gave Danish law to the primitive Anglo-Saxons, and an aristocratic system and architecture to 'Nor-man' France. Their trading settlements brought the beginnings of modern Russia.

The third hegemonic power to revive Europe and drag it out from its abysmal nihilism of child murders, with rape its commonest crime, and prostitutes imported from the east of the continent in their tens of thousands – this power will be that of the millions of Muslims who already live there. They will bring natural religion (Deen al-Fitra), respect for women, safety for children, and the demise of world banking. The restoration of the natural currency of gold and silver.

The new Bedouin will bring to an end the long Revolution that brought to an end the natural system so clearly defined by Ibn Khaldun. They tried to sustain 'a perpetual Revolution'. Once its power had passed from the legislators it continued with the rule of the Sect, the capitalist financial élite. From their point of view the most feared element of this Asabiyya is that the abolition of usury will be the end of the fiduciary contract as their principal instrument of power. The financial aspects of the Bedouin programme imply the necessity of ending banking. To them, this is a Divine Command not an ideology.

Islam, therefore, is already the Nomos that will end the long night of nihilism.

Islam is the natural religion claiming that god is One and nothing associated with Him, and that

Muhammad is the Messenger of Allah. Muslims bless him and ask for peace to be on him.

Earlier it was established that all the great creative spirits who longed for release from nihilism saw that rescue as coming from a couple. The Deen, or life-transaction, is based on the Messenger having been given from the Divine Creator a Revelation to cover for mankind the last phase of human life on the planet. Alongside that Revelation, the Qur'an, there is the life and legal teaching of the Messenger. The principal recorder and guardian of that teaching and legal structure was his beloved wife, Aisha. So important is this that the Muslims say: "Half the Deen from Aisha." Her place after the event of the Revelation is even more crucial, for at the very point that some men wanted to return political rule to a tribal family inheritance, tying the event of Prophecy to one governing family, Aisha with close Companions of the Messenger raised an army to separate Nabawiyat (Prophecy) from political governance. She was successful, and the enemy then created a false religion, uniquely based on a sacred genealogy, called Shi'ism.

A terrorism designated as 'Islamic' was the last attempt by the Sect to sustain itself in power. In practice it followed closely the classical pattern of terrorism, as defined in this text, so that in the end it was not possible to tell what stemmed from a militant anti-American arab movement and what was the fevered invention of secret services. One result of this has been that the true political, social and spiritual nature of Islam has been hidden by a hostile media. It must be borne in mind that no text written in a Muslim country after the fall of the Mughal Dawlet, or after the Khalifate in Istanbul, can be considered valid since written in lands under military and persecutional anti-Islamic regimes.

To conclude the assessment of Ibn Khaldun, six times appointed a judge in the law-courts – here is the vital social dimension of the Islamic identity. Alongside, and as important as the acts of worship – ritual prayers, Ramadan, Zakat and Hajj, Ibn Khaldun considers that the doctrine which charters the social and political nature of a Muslim society is that which defines what man is in Islam. He calls this: Istikhlaf.

This means that man is the guardian of the world.

Allah, the Creator of the Universe has set man on earth to worship Him and to be the Guardian of the world.

To man is given the task of defending the earth, the ocean and the sky, from destruction, pollution and over-exploitation.

He has to answer for the usage of what is on the earth, and under it.

Man's charge is that he must abolish usury – even to a blade of grass.

Man's charge is also the protection of man by the application of the Law.

This demands the abolition of penitentiary punishment and torture, for example, and the execution of rapists and child violators.

This means also a small tax on non-Muslims in Muslim lands, much less than current VAT, to assure their safety and security.

This means the abolition of taxation, except for the commanded poor-tax of Zakat which must be collected, not given.

This means no military conscription by the State.

Now that the indicated Asabiyya has commenced it will be at its strongest and in its fullest meaning, there, where the Sufism is strongest, for it is Sufism that teaches both the science of the self, its patterns of action and choices, and the science of the inner journey to the Lord of the Universe.

Asabiyya is the order of the day. Its success will finish that long period of darkness from 1789. The atheist-bankers' Revolution is at an end.

The restoration of personal rule will follow.

The restoration of Kingship will have been achieved.

The Great Interregnum will be over at last.

The time of the Bedouin has begun.

* * * * *

POSTFACE

From: 'Supplément au roman national'.

"Un jour, un peuple sortira des réduits du 93. Une communauté de destin sorti casquée de l'injustice évoquera ses affinités électives. Le peuple immigré se lèvera enfin. Tout acquis à la Cause. La sortie de la misère se fera donc au nom de l'Islam. Même si la rébellion sera trop neuve pour être récupérée, celle-ci ne peut avoir que le vert pour drapeau. Et tant pis s'ils réclament plus de sexe dans les quartiers. Quel autre drapeau pourrait être le leur? Ils n'ont pas de mémoire ou plutôt mille. De fragiles témoinages de parents que le travail en usine puis dans les services a massacrés. Ils ont autour du cou des chaînes en or avec, en miniature, le trapèze de l'Algerie, le Mali octogone, la forme massive de l'Afrique. Leur besoin d'identité est impossible à rasassier. Ils ont maintenant besoin de se rassembler contre vous. Ils n'ont rien d'autre que l'Islam pour cela.

"Aubervilliers, Stains, Sartrouville, Tremblay-en-France, Bobigny, Aulnay, Mantes-la-Jolie, ces riantes villes de France tomberont. Ils prendront les hôtels de ville, leur merdique pouvoir local, leur apparat d'hommes de bonne volonté. A la fin il n'en restera plus rien. Une libération solitaire des cités-dortoirs pour détruire la division des villes. Ils feront ce que vous attendiez d'eux, dénoueront le malentendu. Rien après ne les empêchera de fondre sur Paris par le pont alexandre-III et d'encercler les Invalides. Rien. Le Quai-d'Orsay sera pris sans offrir de résistance. Il prendrons les symboles. Le métro Charonne. Cognacq-Jay. Le café Drouant. La Place Beauvau. Les boutiques Christian Dior et les monuments aux morts. Des siècles d'accumulation française tomberont entre les mains de la racaille. Et partout les drapeaux verts seront hissés."

Jean-Eric Boulin. (Stock: 2006).

Such would have been the view of the Barbarians held by a Roman governor in Noricum – who could not know that Mozart was coming.

* * * * *

Appendix

DALLAS IN FRANCE

The following paragraph, which appeared in The Times of 25th April 1914, shows that a branch of the family settled in France at an early period.

'A link with the French Revolution has been severed by the death of M. Jean Aristide Dallas, late of Bordeaux, which occurred at his residence, Tamora, Dunedin, New Zealand, on 17th April 1914, at the advanced age of eighty-nine. M. Dallas was the last representative of the French Dallases of Scottish origin, who were people of importance at the Court of Katherine de Médicis. One of M. Dallas's ancestors was a large landed proprietor in Brittany, and took up arms for Louis XVI. For this he, his wife, and family perished at Nantes in "Carrier's Noyades" in 1793. His youngest son escaped, having been harboured by one of his father's tenants, and was restored to his mother's family at Bordeaux when the Revolution was over. His manoir was burnt and his property confiscated, divided up, and sold. His son who escaped Carrier's vengeance had to serve in Napoleon's Grande Armée. He was severely wounded, and retired with the rank of captain.

'M. Dallas was an accomplished linguist and artist, having been taught to paint by Paul Delaroche. He was a friend of Alphonse de Lamartine, and was present with him on the platform when he turned the angry populace from bloodshed by his stirring reference to the French flag, and so saved France another revolution..'

From 'The History of the Family of Dallas and their connections and descendants from the Twelfth Century', by James Dallas.

A NOTE ON THE TYPE

This book was set in Adobe Garamond. Designed for the Adobe Corporation by Robert Slimbach, the fonts are based on types first cut by Claude Garamond (c. 1480–1561). Garamond was a pupil of Geoffroy Tory and is believed to have followed the Venetian models, although he introduced a number of important differences, and it is to him that we owe the letter we now know as "old style". He gave his letters a certain elegance and feeling of movement that won their creator an immediate reputation and the patronage of Francis I of France.